Lean Towards the

Light this Advent &

Christmas

Compiled by Christine Sine
and Lisa DeRosa

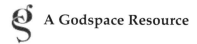

A Godspace Resource

GODSPACE

An Invitation To Create A Pathway To A More Vital Whole-Life Faith

Website: https://godspacelight.com
Email: godspacelight@gmail.com

Cover Design by Hilary Horn

Cover Photograph © Christine Aroney-Sine

ISBN: 9798688893540

Imprint: Independently published

Table of Contents

5

Introduction

Advent marks the beginning of the liturgical year. In the Western church, it starts four Sundays before Christmas Day but Celtic and Orthodox Christians begin the evening of November 15 — forty days before Christmas Day. Celtic Christians always prayed and fasted for forty days in preparation for any major life event, whether it be the planting of a new monastic center or the beginning of a new adventure. Preparation for Christmas was no exception.

I love the Celtic invitation to begin forty days before Christmas Day, before consumerism ramps up to a fever pitch and we become too distracted and overwhelmed by the busyness of the season to really take notice of what matters most. We prepare to celebrate our remembrance of Christ's birth, 2,000 years ago, we prepare to welcome him afresh as saviour in our lives and anticipate his return at the end of time when the fullness of God's redemption will be revealed and all creation will be made new.

Christmas is a twelve-day celebration of this joyful event. It begins on Christmas Day and culminates in the celebration of the Eve of Epiphany which commemorates the coming of the Magi. The beauty of celebrating this entire season is that we usually have it to ourselves. Once Christmas Day is over, Christmas decorations come down and the secular culture finds another focus.

Why Do We Need Advent?

Advent is a challenging season when we await the coming of the promised son of God. Some of us are confused as to what it means. Is it a time to get all of our Christmas shopping done? Or should we be decorating our homes and making Christmas cookies? Or is it a time to plan our Christmas parties?

Advent is meant to remind us of why Christ came, of what is broken in us and our world and why God needed to intervene to bring wholeness. This is a time for deep and serious reflection on how we live our lives and commit ourselves to the purposes of God.

Salvation didn't just happen 2,000 years ago. It is ongoing. It bids us ask – *What do we still need to be saved from? How can our world be made whole again?* Such important questions especially this year as we struggle with issues of climate change, racism and violence, pandemics, economic downturns and the growing recognition of inequalities in our society. We still need to be saved from both our individual and societal sin. We still need to repent and move towards the birth of Christ with a resolve to commit to actions that lead us in a new direction — towards the ways of God, not away from them. Towards healing and love and wholeness, not brokenness and hate and divisiveness.

Advent is also a season of hope. We often forget that the light of Christ is already shining in our world and this brings us to the central question asked in this devotional: *How do we lean into the light of Christ and allow it to shine through us into God's broken world in the coming year?*

In the Northern hemisphere, as we pass through the darkest season of the year, and look towards the coming of the Christ light, we may be aware that darkness is the place in which new seeds germinate. In the Southern hemisphere, where Advent and Christmas are marked by the long days of summer, leaning towards the light might engender images of growth and harvest.

Seeds are planted and grow in the darkness of the soil, just as a baby is planted and grows in the darkness of the womb. The whole season of Advent was designed deliberately to coincide with winter in the Northern hemisphere and Christmas Eve is close to the day of the longest night. Even in the Southern hemisphere where Christmas occurs in the height of summer and nights are short, there is still the sense that each new day emerges out of the night's dark embrace.

We all go through periods of darkness and need seasons like Advent to provide us with hope and promise. *What seeds have been planted and are growing within you? What is slowly emerging and being birthed? How can you nurture these emerging seeds until they are fully birthed to bring light and life to the world as Christ did?*

It is not too early to get ready. Leaning towards the light of Jesus in this season should not just be about going to a few more church services, lighting a few candles or singing carols in the streets. It should be about getting down and doing the things that Jesus would do.

So as we prayerfully move through the season, reading daily reflections, praying and listening for what God is saying to us, there are three questions I would like us to consider:

1. *How can I prepare inwardly for this season and maintain a balanced life that radiates the joy, love and light of Jesus to those I meet?*
2. *How can I reach out to others in ways that will have a lasting effect and enable them to lean in more fully towards the light of Christ?*
3. *How can I ignite the flame in others so that they, too, will radiate the light of Christ?*

This devotional book is divided into five sections. We begin with Celtic Advent and two weeks of preparation. This is a time to think about simplifying, recycling and giving both the earth and yourself a break. The average American will spend over $1,000 on Christmas this year, often giving gifts no one wants and preparing food we would do better not to consume. This year in particular, with the specter of COVID still hanging over all of us, we need to think about alternative ways to celebrate without breaking the bank or quenching our joy. It's hard to put the brakes on but here are some thoughts you might like to consider:

- **Give a gift of fun**. Plan a game night, hold a "make something" Zoom party or special outing like a play date or a visit to your favourite scenic spot with special friends.
- **Plan a gratitude scavenger hunt.** Have each guest wander around their house collecting items they are grateful for. Come together and have each person share three things they have gathered that relate to how Christ has impacted their lives.
- **Go carol singing around the neighbourhood.** When was the last time carol singers came to your door? This is a dying tradition, but one that can be easily adapted to social distancing and it will bring much joy to us and to our neighbours.
- **Have a recycle Christmas.** Most of us have enough leftovers from DIY projects to make something for everyone on our shopping list. Have a DIY party where people bring leftover items to recycle into new projects.

- **Buy locally.** Most of our towns have artisans who would love you to buy their products. Small businesses are struggling to survive and though we may not be able to attend in person, online Christmas fairs are a great place to meet your friends and do your Christmas shopping.
- **Plant a tree (or a forest).** You might want to physically go out and plant trees or donate to an organization that plants trees in devastated and polluted parts of our world.

As traditional Advent begins, the focus of this devotional will shift, but not to the usual Advent themes. We have chosen the following themes for each week:

Week 1: Waiting in Silence
Week 2: Waiting for a Vulnerable God
Week 3: Living In Hope
Week 4: Lean Towards the Light

May this be a blessed Advent and Christmas season for you. May you lean towards the light so that you can come closer to the Christ child and be better prepared to radiate the love of God in the coming year.

Christine Sine

CELTIC ADVENT:

Preparing Our Hearts

A Celtic Advent – The Creative Breath

by John Birch

We begin our journey with this Celtic style liturgy that you might like to adapt at other steps of your journey.

Symbols: A large candle and beneath it, a bowl of water

The candle is lit.

(A few moments of silence)

 (Read John 1:1-3, Genesis 1:2)

Lord of the morning
of dawn chorus
rising sun
mist on water

Lord of the noontime
of chattering voices
laughter and fun
sparkling water
everyone

Lord of the evening
of quiet breeze
setting sun
gentle waters
day that's done

O Lord, our Lord
How majestic is your name in all the earth
You have set your glory above the heavens
And from the lips of children ordained praise
 O Lord, our Lord
How majestic is your name in all the earth

Creative God, breath of all life
Through whom all things
are created and sustained;
all sons and daughters
flocks and herds,
all birds of the air
and fish of the sea
You walked this earth
as child and Creator
You touched the soil
quenched your thirst
embraced this world
brought life and light
love and laughter
into dark and death-filled lives
Creative God, breath of all life
Through whom all things
are created and sustained
We bring to you our sacrifice
of a contrite and willing heart
O come, Thou Wisdom from on high,
Who orders all things mightily;
To us the path of knowledge show,
And teach us in her ways to go.

Rejoice! Rejoice! Emmanuel
Shall come again and with us ever dwell

(A space for music to be played or sung — a Taizé chant would be
most appropriate)

(Read Psalm 20:6-8)

(A moment of silence – During the silence, you may like to read and
reflect on the words that have been read, gaze at the candle — or
simply enjoy the peace and calm.)

May this eternal truth be always on our hearts
That the God who breathed this world into being
Placed stars into the heavens
And designed a butterfly's wing
Is the God who entrusted his life
to the care of ordinary people
became vulnerable that we might know
how strong is the power of Love
A mystery so deep it is impossible to grasp
A mystery so beautiful it is impossible to ignore

(Scripture reading — possibly the Gospel reading for the day)

(A space for a hymn or song to be sung/said)

(Intercessions – A circle prayer. Imagine throwing a pebble into the centre of a pond, and the circles of ripples that move out from the centre.)

We pray firstly for those closest to us, our immediate family and closest friends — for their health, needs, joys and fears.
(Silent prayer)
and fears.
(Silent prayer)
God of creation, God of Salvation
Hear the prayers of our hearts

We pray for our extended family and friends who we might not see each week — for their love and concern, for their wellbeing.
(Silent prayer)
God of creation, God of Salvation
Hear the prayers of our hearts

As the ripples reach out toward the land we pray for those who we only have contact with annually or less — for a blessing this Advent-time

(Silent prayer)
God of creation, God of Salvation
Hear the prayers of our hearts

And as the ripples reach their furthest point we pray for this world
and its people — for the needs of this week and the future.
(Silent prayer)
God of creation, God of Salvation
Who speaks to us through thunder and whisper
Who loves us as if there were but one of us to love
Hear the prayers of our hearts

Lord, thou hast given us thy Word for a light to shine upon our path;
grant us so to meditate on that Word, and to follow its teaching,
that we may find in it the light that shines more and more until the
perfect day; through Jesus Christ our Lord. (Jerome, c 342 – 420)[1]

*John is a Methodist Local Preacher based on the South coast of Wales, and
also a writer, mainly of prayers and Bible studies, either accessed through his
website www.faithandworship.com, FaceBook page or via several published
books. Some of these prayers have been used in choral works, and translated
into other languages. When not writing, or playing guitar, you'll find John
and his wife Margaret exploring the coastal paths of Wales and further afield,
and both are very keen birdwatchers!*

Set Your Heart in the Right Direction

by Christine Sine

Welcome to Celtic Advent.

"As we begin this journey of Advent start by setting your heart in the right direction."[2] As I read this starting reflection in David Cole's excellent Celtic Advent devotional book, I realized how much I need to set my own heart in the right direction. Focusing on Advent and the coming of Christ as the intention of my heart and soul isn't always easy but I know it is extremely important. So as we begin this Advent journey, I encourage you, too, to set your heart in the right direction by joining me in the middle of November for the beginning of Celtic Advent.

For Orthodox Christians, this is a time of fasting, not as strict as the Lenten fast, but a fast nonetheless, when adherents refrain from meat, dairy, fish, wine, and olive oil. Whether we fast or not, Advent and especially this extended Celtic Advent, is a time to prepare for the great feast we celebrate at the birth of Christ by shifting our focus from ourselves to others. This is a season when we should worry less about what we eat, when we eat and how much we eat in order to free up time for prayer and caring of others. As individuals, we can honor the fast, spend more time in prayer, and make a conscious effort to love our neighbors as ourselves, dedicating this season to be a time for true, spiritual growth.

To help me move in this direction, a couple of years ago, I used the theme *I choose joy* for the whole season of Advent. As I usually do at the beginning of Advent, I put together an Advent garden, deliberately choosing a circular bowl to plant my succulents in as a reminder of the circle of my life. I also chose to recycle plants from a previous garden, this too, a reminder that the circle of my life is not new but can be refreshed and replanted so that what is inside gives me greater joy. I painted rocks with a word that represented my weekly themes and then added candles that I lit each week in lieu of an Advent wreath.

I choose joy may seem like a strange theme for a season of fasting or of simplifying which has traditionally been my focus in preparing for

Christmas, but as I read in *The Book of Joy* by Archbishop Desmond Tutu and The Dalai Lama, "Joy is a way of approaching the world."[3] Our greatest joy comes when we reframe our situation more positively, experience gratitude and choose to be kind and generous. In a nutshell, our greatest joy comes when we focus away from ourselves and seek to do good for others.

So let's begin our celebration of Advent this year, with a few simple questions. Find a piece of paper or choose a fresh page in your journal. Write the words *I choose joy* on the page. Spend a few minutes prayerfully considering this phrase.

Now turn to a fresh page and draw a circle. Write inside the circle all the responsibilities and activities that you expect will consume your time in the coming weeks. What in your circle gives you joy? Highlight these responsibilities with a brightly coloured marker or crayon. What are you choosing that gives God joy? Highlight these with another coloured marker.

Now prayerfully look at your list and consider how you could reshape your time over the coming weeks to increase your joy and be kind and generous towards others. *What do you need to let go of to increase your joy? What do you need to add and how will that reshape your preparations for Christmas?*

Christine describes herself as a contemplative activist, passionate gardener, author, and liturgist. She is the founder of Godspace and her most recent book is The Gift of Wonder: Creative Practices for Delighting in God.

Preparing Our Hearts & Homes

by Andy Wade

Rip! Another calendar page bites the dust. November is upon us and the stores are already crammed with Christmas decorations. Even before Halloween we were bombarded with Christmas and Thanksgiving items ready to be snatched up by the all-too-easily-influenced consumer.

All this reminds me why we chose to focus November on preparing our hearts and homes for Advent and Christmas. We need to be proactive. It's not just the temptation to be swept up by the marketing machine; the pace of our lives seem to keep time with the hustle and bustle of the holidays. Before we know it, it's January 1 and we're making resolutions to do better next Christmas.

Resistance Is Futile! (or is it?)

"Overcoming Consumerism": What can we do to resist the onslaught? First and foremost, we need to be intentional. Most often I think we acknowledge the craziness of the season, wish it were different, then plunge in without a plan.

Begin your week asking:

- *What are the temptations to overconsume this coming week? Why am I tempted by them?* (Knowing what motivates us to overconsume is a deeply spiritual issue.) *How can I become more aware of my unhealthy motivations as I go about my week?*
- *What gives me peace? What can I do this week that will help me to rest and refocus?* You might create a place of rest in or around your home. You might try setting an alarm on your phone to 9:00 am, 12:00 noon, 3:00 pm, 6:00 pm, and 9:00 pm — simple reminders to stop, pray, and rest for a moment in God. Perhaps you could change how you take lunch, turning that time into a sacred break in the middle of your day.
- *In the week ahead, where am I tempted to make things complicated?* For many, Advent and Christmas are times to go overboard on

decorations, lavish treats and dinners, and packed schedules. Take time to reflect on what is most important. If helpful, reframe your gatherings from entertainment to a gathering of good friends. When we focus on entertaining, or even hospitality, we often end up emphasizing the production rather than the people. *How can you simplify by cultivating good conversations and relationships rather than complex party plans?*

- That last point leads right into making space for hospitality. For us introverts, this may unearth anxieties about crowds and chaos during this season, especially as COVID continues to keep many of us isolated. But hospitality comes in many shapes and sizes. Valuing friendships over frenzy, you might make a point of meeting each week for coffee or tea with one person who is important to you. It might be the same person every week, or you might choose to meet with different people.

You might also want to facilitate a small gathering of friends, potluck dinner and/or have a cookie exchange. Invite friends over for a game night, or how about a movable decoration party where you turn putting up those outdoor lights into a rotating group event? The point is to get people together in simple, fun ways that emphasize togetherness… with good social distancing, of course.

At the end of the week, turn those questions inside-out by asking yourself:

- *How well did I live into my goals?*
- *What can I do differently this coming week?*
- *Who can I invite to join me on this journey?*

That last question is critical for most of us: On our own, we're often not too successful at change. We need others around us. We need people to ask how we're doing, what difficulties we're facing as the holidays near, and to journey with us into a more Christ-focused season. Who might that be for you?

I hope you join us on this expedition through the jungle of holiday excess. Many perils may cross our path, but together we can reach our destination in peace and with sanity in-tact.

One more thing you might find is that journaling will help you to better arrange your thoughts and review your progress. Journals don't have to be written, they might be drawn, painted, or a scrapbook of reminders. If you do choose to write, think about different forms of writing that might release even more reflection — try a poem, a short story, or even a song.

Andy Wade is the facilitator for M25 the Gorge focusing on immigrant/ immigration issues and walking with our Latinx neighbors. He serves on the Gorge Ecumenical Ministries board and lives in Hood River, OR with his wife, Susan.

A Place of Utter Delight

by Christine Sine

"The Eternal God planted a garden in the East in Eden—*a place of utter delight*—and placed the man whom He had sculpted there. *In this garden,* He made the ground pregnant *with life—bursting forth* with nourishing food and *luxuriant* beauty. *He created* trees, and in the center of this garden *of delights* stood the tree of life and the tree of the knowledge of good and evil" (Genesis 2:8-9 The Voice).

Celtic Christians believed that creation was translucent and that the glory of God shone through it, so as I take inspiration from Celtic Advent this year, it isn't surprising that I want to spend a good chunk of time reflecting on creation. Predictably, it was Genesis 2:8-9 that came to mind, and especially this beautiful translation. God created our world to be a "place of utter delight" where all created life flourishes and praises God with its luxuriant beauty. God's delight, God's joy is a flourishing creation bursting forth with nourishing food and luxuriant beauty. It is good to remind ourselves of this as we move towards Christmas and the joy of Christ's birth.

How do we ensure that this garden of delight that God desires to see whole and healthy, flourishes, I wonder? It seems that we do more to destroy and pollute it than to preserve and grow it.

As I thought about this, the circle motif came to my mind. This symbol of wholeness and completeness is repeated over and over again in nature. It is as though it stands as a constant reminder of God's desire for wholeness and flourishing. So I decided to create a succulent mandala. Like many of my friends, I have become a little obsessed with succulents lately and part of that passion is seeing how many of them I can propagate from leaves, hence the succulent mandala. My hope was that they would, in the next couple of months, burst into life and luxuriant beauty.

The circle of the mandala is symbolic for me of the circle of our world. It, too, is meant to be whole and pregnant with life; a place where we plant, nurture and grow with expectant joy and anticipation until all is flourishing and fruitful. I chose as many different shapes and colours as I could to create my mandala, reminding myself of the rich diversity of God's creation. At the centre was a succulent that had already begun to grow, symbolic of the tree of life at the centre of God's garden. As I spread out my succulent leaves, I prayed for the places and people in our world devastated by the impact of climate change. I prayed for those who work to reverse this devastation and I prayed, too, for those who are indifferent to it.

I reflected on the God who created that first garden with such obvious joy and I wonder what we can do as we celebrate this God coming into our world in the person of Jesus Christ, to preserve, grow and encourage flourishing. As I thought about this, I added a string of pearl succulents around the centre, reminding me of the pearl of great value whose birthday we are soon to celebrate.

You may not be into succulents, but I am sure that there is some way that you can connect to God's garden of utter delight at this season. Pause for a few minutes to consider what you could do. You might like to use the suggestions below to stir your own creativity.

So many of our Christmas symbols are from the natural world — wreaths and trees, holly and mistletoe. Here are some thoughts on how to connect to God's garden world and grow you joy in creation as Christ's birth approaches.

- **Visit a Christmas tree farm** with your family or friends and bring home a live tree, or better yet, consider a living tree that you can either keep for many years to come or plant out in your garden as an ongoing reminder of God's love of creation.
- **Create a living wreath for your house.** Succulents are great for this, though pine branches and cones also make an excellent wreath that will survive well throughout the season. In the Southern hemisphere, poinsettias, waratahs, or proteas would be good alternatives.
- **Plant bulbs** either inside, like Amaryllis, or outside in expectation of daffodils, tulips and crocuses bursting through the soil in a couple of months.
- **Visit an outdoor Advent spiral or labyrinth or Christmas tree lighting.** So much of what we do at this season, at least in the Northern hemisphere, tends to be inside. Consider ways that you can take some of the celebrations of Christmas outside this year.

Perhaps we can even learn from our Southern hemisphere friends, many of whom will spend Christmas on the beach. A good walk along a windswept beach is energizing and at least for me, pregnant with the joy of Christmas.

Christine describes herself as a contemplative activist, passionate gardener, author, and liturgist. She is the founder of Godspace and her most recent book is The Gift of Wonder: Creative Practices for Delighting in God.

Finding Rhythm in Advent

by Lilly Lewin

Advent is a great time to put rhythm into your life, and Celtic Advent started on November 15. I like starting Advent early because it allows me the time to prepare Him Room! Advent allows me the time to prepare my heart for the arrival of Jesus! The Celtic Christians and Orthodox Christians allow forty days to prepare for the Nativity, just like Lent is forty days of preparation before Easter. What kind of rhythm do you need in your life as the holidays begin?

Rhythm is a part of God's creation… a part of how God designed the universe.

Day and night

Sun and moon

Changing of the seasons.

All of these help us remember and help us have time and space in our daily routine to rest, reflect, listen, remember, rejoice and worship the Creator.

Sadly, our culture in the West, especially America, has forgotten rhythm. And sadly, we've corrupted the rest of the world with our 24/7 mentality. We expect to be able to shop, eat out, and see movies whenever we want. We don't expect to rest… so we don't. We have been taught that a full calendar means you are successful. And REST is not valued.

And, especially during the holidays, we want to have our calendars filled with parties and events so no one gets bored. What if that's not the best way according to the Creator? What if God had something better in mind from the first days of the world? God set up the rhythm of the world… six days creating and one day resting. Who says we are bigger and know better than God?

What would happen if we made REST and RHYTHM parts of our Advent practice this year? What would that even look like? What would you need to add in or subtract from your calendar in order to find rhythm before Christmas this year?

How could you practice slowing down and finding rhythm rather than living into the crazy busyness of the season? How would you practice REST in the midst of the holidays?

Some ideas to try:

Take a Walk: Something as simple as taking a walk could add rhythm and rest to your day. And a walk can be done with your dog, your spouse, your roommate, a friend and/or with your kids. And not just taking a walk for exercise, but taking a walk to connect with God. Taking a walk to be with Jesus outside, in Creation. Take a walk and take time to notice what is going on in nature. Notice the plants, the sky, the birds, and even the bugs along the way! Take time to BREATHE!

Take a Nap: Actually, TAKE A NAP. I saw a plaque at a craft show that said, "Jesus took Naps, I want to be like Jesus!" (Mark 4:38) What if we actually allowed ourselves the time to take a nap. When my kids were little ,I would try to get as much done as possible while they slept. Now, I think the healthier thing to do might be to take a nap too! Or even just give yourself permission to lie down on the couch or your bed for fifteen minutes with no agenda! Just to be. I believe REST is holy so taking fifteen minutes would be taking holy time! Taking a nap like Jesus even in the middle of the holiday storm!

Take Time to Light a Candle: Many of us create or use Advent wreaths during Advent. The traditional Advent wreath consists of a circle of evergreen greenery (representing eternal life and eternity) and four candles to be lit one at a time, adding a candle each week as the weeks go on. On Christmas, a white center candle is often added as the Christ candle to signify Jesus's birth. There are various meanings for the candles. I grew up with the candles meaning Prophet, Bethlehem, Shepherd, and Angel, but some traditions have the candles represent Hope, Peace, Joy and Love. Some church traditions use three purple candles (purple is the liturgical color for Advent signifying royalty) and one pink (week 3 for Joy), but I tend to use four dark red candles just because I like that better than purple and pink! I have also used all white candles, too. I also saw a fun centerpiece at Target that I might use this year for something different, candles in a row rather than in the round.

If you choose to start Advent early, you might create something different for the first two weeks and then go to the more traditional Advent wreath on the first Sunday of Advent. One year, I started with fall colors before traditional Advent began, then took out the brown ones, removed the leaves and left the dark green for my wreath. Last week, we created a **centerpiece of Thankfulness**. We lit the candles for things we are thankful for. I filled a container with sand and then used birthday candles for our prayer candles. We are doing this as a reminder to be grateful as we approach Thanksgiving here in the States.

Even more simply, you might just **add a single candle to your day.** Light a candle with your coffee cup or your cup of tea as a way to pause and create rhythm in your day. Taking time to consider how you might prepare your heart for Jesus and his birth. Or you might light a candle when the kids finish school for the day and take a couple of minutes to thank God. Have the kids take turns lighting the candle or candles and saying what they are thankful for today, or where they felt God's love during the day. This could be a great practice before homework begins.

How would you like to add rhythm and rest to your life this Advent? What will you discover as you walk, nap, and light candles in the weeks to come?

Lilly is a worship curator, speaker, author, artist, and founder of thinplaceNASHVILLE, and freerangeworship.com She creates sacred space prayer experiences and leads workshops & retreats across the country and beyond. She writes the freerangefriday blog each week at Godspacelight.com

An Unexpected Symbol of Advent

by April Yamasaki

For Christmas last year I received an amaryllis bulb—the kind that's shipped in a box with the premixed soil, plastic pot, and step-by-step instructions. Just as directed, I planted the bulb up to its neck in the potting soil and placed the pot in a warm spot with good light. The stem had already started growing while still in the box, so I watered the soil lightly and hoped the pale growth would turn green as it grew.

The stem did grow and green up a bit, but then it seemed to lose heart. It was too weak to stand up straight and soon had bent double. I hoped a second stem might emerge to produce bright red flowers like the ones shown on the box, but as it turned out I hoped in vain. All I got were leaves—so healthy, dark green, and long and longer that they stretched out beyond the tabletop, and lasted until the end of October.

I'm disappointed that my amaryllis bulb didn't flower, but I hope the vigor of its leaves allowed it to store up energy enough to bloom this year. At least that's what I hope for as my bulb is resting now in a cool, dark closet. Soon it will be time to pot it in fresh soil, bring it into the light, and place it in a warm spot. Will a stem emerge healthy and strong this time? Will there be flowers standing at the top like a brilliant red crown? Or is my green thumb only for the leaves?

This year my amaryllis bulb is my unexpected symbol of Advent. It reminds me that far from being passive, waiting takes some tending. Waiting means watching in expectation. Sometimes waiting leads to more waiting. Just as I wait again in expectation of amaryllis flowers, we are again waiting for Christmas, just as we did last year and the year before and the years before that. We wait for the fullness of time to celebrate the coming of Christ the King.

For some Christians in the early church, the expectation of Christ's return was so strong and so immediate that they stopped working. Why work to build a house when the Lord will come before you have time to finish? Why work in the fields, when the Lord will come before the harvest? Why bother to make a living when the end is so near? Why not just sit and wait?

And so they sat idle—and became a burden to those in their community who continued to work. To address this, 2 Thessalonians 3:10-13 gave these instructions:

For even when we were with you, we gave you this rule: "The one who is unwilling to work shall not eat." We hear that some among you are idle and disruptive. They are not busy; they are busybodies. Such people we command and urge in the Lord Jesus Christ to settle down and earn the food they eat. And as for you, brothers and sisters, never tire of doing what is good.

So while I'm waiting for my amaryllis to bloom, while we're waiting for Christ the King at Christmas and in the fullness of time, I'm taking these words to heart. Let us do the work that God has set before us and never tire of doing good.

April Yamasaki is an ordained minister who currently serves as resident author with a liturgical worship community, and speaks widely in churches and other settings. She is the author of Four Gifts; Seeking Self-Care for Heart, Soul, Mind, and Strength and other books on Christian living. For more information, see her websites: Writing and Other Acts of Faith and When You Work for the Church: the good, the bad, and the ugly, and how we can all do better.

Making Christianity Unfamiliar Again

by Christine Sine

Let us go forth today,
In the love of our Creator,
In the strength of our Redeemer,
In the power of our Sustainer,
In the fellowship of witness
From every tribe and nation and culture.
Let us go forth today,
United with the Sacred Three,
In harmony with the Holy One
Compassion in our hearts,
Gratitude in our thoughts,
Generosity in our deeds,
Justice as our passion.
Let us go forth today,
Carrying God's image
Into our hurting world.[4]

In the US, traditional Advent usually begins just after Thanksgiving. Many of us set up our Advent wreaths, light our first Advent candle and begin to read our Advent devotionals. Some of us buy Christmas trees and decorate them.

Last year, I decided to take a different approach. I was reading Heidi Haverkamp's *Advent in Narnia* and was deeply impacted by her introductory words: "Lewis, by placing Christianity into another world, makes it unfamiliar again. He gives us the chance to feel a newfound wonder at the depth of God's love, the power of Christ's grace and the totality of his sacrifice and the wonder of a world infused with the Holy Spirit."[5]

I love the idea of making Advent unfamiliar again, and in 2020 when I was writing this, COVID-19 made Christmas unfamiliar for all of us; something that we can either resent or embrace.

So, I invite you to embrace with me this journey into an unfamiliar story, the unfamiliar story of Jesus' birth as it was without all the glamour of Christmas lights and carols and presents. So often we look at Advent from God's side of the story — the angel Gabriel's visit, virgin birth, the choirs of angels singing at Christ's birth. Or, we think of the cultural images we see on Christmas cards — a beautiful looking stable surrounded by a few animals and very well-dressed shepherds. This Advent, I am thinking about an unfamiliar Jesus – the human story of unwed mothers, supportive cousins, and welcoming surrogate fathers. What does Advent look like through their eyes? What does it look like through Jesus' eyes — this vulnerable, possibly even despised and rejected, child from birth?

We know very little about Jesus' childhood and the characteristics he displayed but we do know quite a bit about his birth and those who surrounded and nurtured him. What we know should stir a lot of emotions and raise a lot of questions for us.

Why did God choose such a vulnerable, young woman to give birth to the Messiah? How did Joseph feel? What was it like to be a refugee in his day and age? Jesus may have been vulnerable and possibly even rejected and despised from birth, yet he was obviously also loved not just by Mary, but also by her husband, Joseph, who kept both of them safe through an arduous journey as refugees into Egypt. Were they part of a refugee caravan like we seen moving across Mexico each year? How were they treated in Egypt?

It was writing *The Gift of Wonder* and developing resources like Advent gardens[6] that encouraged me to step outside the box into an unfamiliar view of Advent and, in fact, of the whole gospel story. The story of Jesus' conception and birth raises some challenging and uncomfortable questions for us. How can we become like THIS child and what his birth tells us about the God that we follow? Fully human, yet fully God. Powerful, yet vulnerable. Loved, yet rejected. What does it mean to you?

God bless you in this unsettling season of waiting as we move towards our remembrance of Christ's birth.

Christine describes herself as a contemplative activist, passionate gardener, author, and liturgist. She is the founder of Godspace and her most recent book is The Gift of Wonder: Creative Practices for Delighting in God.

Grieving on Black Friday

by Lilly Lewin

The day after Thanksgiving is called Black Friday here in the States. I don't know if this event takes place in other parts of the world, but here in America, Black Friday is one of the biggest shopping days of the year. It's so big that some stores choose to open on Thursday night! That means opening at the end of a national holiday, Thanksgiving. We've just spent a day, supposedly being grateful for what we have, but then our culture encourages us to go out and spend money on things we think we need or we hope will bring us joy and happiness! The contrast between the two days is stark. I tend to avoid Black Friday altogether. It's actually been a spiritual practice to avoid all shopping on Black Friday. It's hard to do when all the ads on TV and in email are advertising the "great deals" that you don't want to miss! There is so much intensity about shopping and getting stuff that it grieves my soul.

Black Friday has me thinking of grief in general. As I was getting ready to host my family for Thanksgiving, I was praying for all the families in California who lost their homes and couldn't gather around their tables this year. I thought about everyone who lost family members and friends in the California fires. I thought about all people I know who are celebrating their first big holiday without a loved one, parent, spouse, or child. There is pain in the process of going about the day and all the memories of those people and traditions.

I've also been grieving the US vs THEM mentality in our country. Here in America, we are divided about so many things. We just had a major election and this did not make us more connected, but rather showed us how deeply we are entrenched on our sides. Hatred and lack of compassion seem to be seeping into all areas of our lives. We seem to have forgotten the golden rule of doing unto others as we would have them do unto us. We seem to abandon the greatest commandments to love God and love our neighbor.

How do we move forward? What can we do?

31

I think we need to acknowledge our grief in order to move forward! We need to acknowledge our pain and allow God to begin to heal it. Grief about the world, our country and the pain and grief in our personal lives.

As we move into the season of Advent, where we prepare our hearts for the coming of Jesus, let's let the Light of Jesus shine into the darkness that we are carrying around with us.

I went to the National Youth Workers Convention in St. Louis, MO where over 4,000 youth workers from all over the country gathered to learn and be encouraged in their ministries. As a part of the Soul Care Team, we created space for these folks to get their cups filled up, not just "get more information". There were spiritual directors, the Prayer Chapel filled with Prayer Stations, and I curated the Sanctuary where we taught prayer practices like centering prayer, Benedictine spirituality, Sabbath, and pray the hours. My friend, Beth Slevcove, lead a workshop on grief. She has a great book on learning to grieve called *Broken Hallelujahs: Learning to Grieve the Big and Small Losses of Life*.

We also had a prayer station in the Chapel that allowed folks to process their grief. People wrote down the things that they were grieving and tied these prayers onto a grapevine.

Grief…

Blessed are those who mourn…

WRITE your prayers of grief and regret on a piece of muslin then tie it to the grapevine.

Give your loss, grief, despair to Jesus, The True Vine.

What things are weighing you down?

What losses have you experienced this year?

What pain, grief, despair are you carrying with you right now?

What do you need to take time to grieve before Advent?

Make a list and give it to Jesus.

Perhaps you need to burn this list and let it go in that way.

Maybe you need to create a wailing wall of some kind and place your prayers of grief on the wall and give them to Jesus to hold and heal.

Maybe you just need to set aside some time to write in your journal or take a walk and talk to Jesus about your pain.

Take time this Black Friday to honor yourself and your grief. Be still. Be real. Jesus knows our hearts already and longs to bring us hope and comfort in our sorrow.

Let's allow Jesus to prepare room in our hearts as we prepare for his incarnation.

Lilly is a worship curator, speaker, author, artist, and founder of thinplaceNASHVILLE, and freerangeworship.com She creates sacred space prayer experiences and leads workshops & retreats across the country and beyond. She writes the freerangefriday blog each week at Godspacelight.com

Surrounded by the Embrace of God

by Christine Sine

Just before Advent, I like to reorganize my sacred space where I do my devotions each morning. I like to set up a circle of candles around me. As I light them each day, I sense a special connection to the people, places and things that I feel God's circle of light, revealed in the coming of Christ, embraces for me. As I light the candle in front of a family photo, I thank God for the light that surrounds my family and friends. I progress from there to a candle surrounded by air plants. That connects me to the circle of God's creation without which there would be no life on this planet. Then the candle on my altar, reminding me that God's circle of light embraces all that is sacred and special in our world. From there to my office desk – God's light embraces my work, and last but not least, my "I choose joy" Advent garden where I sense the divine presence in all the inhabitants of our planet.

I sit in the middle of this circle, surrounded by the wonder of God's love. I thank God for the circle of divine presence which embraces not just me and my family, but my neighbours near and far. In fact, it embraces all the peoples of the earth past, present and future. It embraces those who have lost homes to the pandemic, as well as to hurricanes, floods and fires this year. It embraces those who have fled from war, conflict and violence. It embraces those of us who have warm and comfortable homes to dwell in and abundant food to eat. It embraces those who live in poverty and in wealth. People from every race, nation and strata of society.

What I love about the circle of God's light is that it excludes no one and nothing. God's light, the Christ child who comes to us at Christmas, welcomes all of us into the circle of God's family, inviting us to surrender not just to the loving embrace of our God, but also to the embrace of each other. God's circle of light invites us to find unity and learn to care for each other as one global family.

Lord, I sit in this circle of light,

surrounded by your love,
embraced by your peace,
infused with your joy.
Lord, I sit in this circle of light,
with all the people of this world
secure in the wonder of your presence.

*Christine describes herself as a contemplative activist, passionate gardener,
author, and liturgist. She is the founder of Godspace and her most recent book
is The Gift of Wonder: Creative Practices for Delighting in God.*

Simplifying Advent and Christmas

by Andy Wade

Confession time: I'm not much of a planner. I know how to plan and can do it quite effectively when it comes to my work, but daily living? I'd rather fly by the seat of my pants. If that sounds exciting, well, for an introvert, it usually just means hanging around the house and puttering in the garden.

That's why what I'm about to say may come as a shock to those who know me best. One of the best ways to simplify Advent and Christmas is to plan ahead. Even as I write those words, I can feel my body tense up. For me, this idea is completely counter-intuitive. Let's relax and just play the holidays by ear, is my inclination.

I've learned over the years that "playing it by ear" over the holidays doesn't work so well. With all the parties, events, expectations, and obligations, this approach ends up leading to more stress. Planning ahead sets limits I can be comfortable with. Yes, I'll have to negotiate those limits with my much more outgoing spouse, but together we can find balance.

What are your favorite Advent and Christmas events? How can you plan ahead to make sure they are simple and low-stress? How could you adapt these with social distancing?

Do you like cookies around the house during the holidays? When our children were younger, we celebrated St. Nicholas' Day (Dec. 6). We would bake several different kinds of cookies ahead of time and wake up to a "taste of Christmas" on St. Nicholas' Day: candles filling the table and room, St. Nicholas' stockings, and plates filled with one or two of each kind of cookie.

I remember also the stress of needing to get cookies made because the day had snuck up on us and we were unprepared. Some years, we prepared well, other years not so much. But what if we shared this idea with friends, got together for an evening of games, and talked about our favorite Christmas cookies. We could then each plan on making an extra-large batch of our favorite cookie and come back together in a week for a cookie exchange. Presto! I baked one or two kinds of cookies and ended up with a wide variety of my friends' favorites! Planning ahead just became fun and simplified my life without sacrificing tradition.

Do you give presents at Christmas? Are there ways you can cut out or cut down the shopping and opt for home-made gifts?

In the past few years, I've created a photo calendar for my family. With online tools, it's both easy and affordable. But I've also tended to wait until the last minute. I've made calendars for my wife's side of the family and for my side. Each calendar is personalized for the family with birthdays, anniversaries, and other important dates.

Planning ahead actually makes this a fun experience with time to reflect and pray for each family member as I collect the dates and enter them onto the calendar. Failing to plan ahead results in stress or just abandoning the project and settling for store-bought presents.

Do you like to host parties? How might you collaborate to turn planning and prep into a time of celebration with friends? This year you might like to try something different like a learning party over Zoom where you collaborate together to make mozzarella cheese or Scottish shortbread.

My parents love to host parties. For many years, they partnered with close friends to host a New Year's Eve party. One year at my parents' home, the next at the Cromptons'. They planned together and hosted together, which made the event much easier and more fun. Too often we think that if a party is at our house then we need to do all the work. That's simply not true!

Find some friends, share the load and enjoy the laughs. Simplifying Advent and Christmas can be fun!

Andy Wade is the facilitator for M25 the Gorge focusing on immigrant/ immigration issues and walking with our Latinx neighbors. He serves on the Gorge Ecumenical Ministries board and lives in Hood River, OR with his wife, Susan.

Preparing for the Gift of a Baby

by Lilly Lewin

This past weekend was our first taste of fall here in Tennessee. The ninety-degree weather finally broke with a weekend of rain and a fresh breath of cold wind so that we now wake to temps in the mid-forties and highs in the low sixties. Much better for my soul than the extended heat and humidity of this year. I'm just getting used to the idea of harvest and pumpkins on my porch. I even have a large pumpkin growing in my side yard. It's a gift pumpkin from the seeds of last year's jack-o-lantern that planted itself. I'm looking for more gifts in my world at the moment. Unexpected gifts like side yard pumpkins, cardinals on the mailbox, a postcard from an old friend. It's been a long year of world problems and political battling. Just turning on the news can turn up my stress level. I need the gift of peace and the gift of pausing. I need the reminder that God is still in control and God's Light still shines brightly even when it feels dark. And I need the Hope of new life that can be found in the arrival of a baby.

We are all waiting for the gift of Light to arrive. We all need two new eyes to see the gifts and light around us. We all can prepare our hearts for the gift of Baby Jesus and the celebration of his arrival.

How can you get ready for the gift of Jesus this year?

When a baby is coming, there is a lot to do, lots to plan for and special gear to acquire in order to be ready for the baby's arrival.

What things need to happen in order for you to prepare Him room?

Do you need to clear your calendar?

Do you need to make a plan?

Do you need to prepare mentally or change your attitude?

What does this look like?

Talk to God about this.

Can you get ready for the gift of Jesus as a baby, a baby who needs our time and attention? Are we willing to accept this and receive Jesus as an infant? How are you willing to change your life in order to give baby Jesus the attention and care he needs? Consider this today.

Talk to God about how you can receive and prepare for Baby Jesus!

You might want to buy some baby supplies like a baby bottle, or diapers, or a bottle of baby lotion to have on hand as symbolic reminders that the Light of the World is being born and it's time to prepare for his arrival. Put on some baby lotion. Let the smell remind you to prepare for the gift of the Baby Jesus. Take time to receive the Gift of Baby Jesus!

Lilly is a worship curator, speaker, author, artist, and founder of thinplaceNASHVILLE, and freerangeworship.com She creates sacred space prayer experiences and leads workshops & retreats across the country and beyond. She writes the freerangefriday blog each week at Godspacelight.com

5 Steps to a Meaningful Christmas Season

by John Lewis

Putting up lights or stockings, baking cookies, and wrapping presents may be JOY-FILLED traditions your family already practices. TRADITIONS can help connect these familiar practices and symbols of the Christmas story to your family's heritage, values, faith and personality. Year after year, these require a higher degree of intentionality. While many of us may not have grown up with traditions like that, their BLESSINGS are much worth the effort and planning! Where do we start? The most enduring FAITH traditions (Lord's Supper, Baptism, Weddings) are practiced in community. So, we know that relying on others is a tried and true place to start. Carissa and I offer below not a formula but some steps that might help your family create and celebrate meaningful family CHRISTMAS traditions.

Step #1: Decide to do it

Let's face it. There are many obstacles during the holidays that must be overcome to achieve meaningful and faith-filled Christmas traditions: busyness, distraction, guilt, and added Christmas duties during the month. So:

- Gather your family to discuss the benefits of traditions together (family bonding and identity, passing down values and faith, etc.). If you decide together, you will set yourself up for success.
- Decide as parents and as a family that this is important. Declare that with God's help, you will start some small but meaningful traditions. Ironically, the best time to start is when your kids are young, when you are still scrambling and the kids seem too young to understand much. They will pick up more than we realize.
- Pray for God's help and commit this to God together. It's not about you being responsible for their success!

Step #2: Start with brainstorming

- Identify any traditions for your families of origin that you want to continue or adapt (putting up the tree/lights, e.g.)? What does your family already love to do together during Christmas?

40

- Identify some family values, Christmas stories, and biblical themes you want to highlight this Christmas season (giving, serving, e.g.).
- Identify your family's passions, practices, and personality. What do you already like to do? (love for baking, e.g.) These might contribute ideas to adapting old Christmas traditions or starting new ones.

Step #3: Find some resources

- Resources that identify the original story, legend, meaning behind the symbols and traditions of Christmas.
- Books or guides that you can use, learn from, or adapt for building meaningful long term traditions (I could not easily find one that I liked that would suit this purpose, so I did my own.)
- Ask for help from others who either already practice holiday traditions, or who might be willing to try new traditions with you-together in person and/or through technology.

Step #4: Make your plan

- Create your tradition as a couple and whenever possible, as a whole family. Be specific but not rigid about the what, when, where and how of practicing your traditions. Mark your family calendar.
- Do the traditions fit both your family and the hopes you have for passing on values and faith?
- Start small. Make the plan doable. It's better to do something for five minutes than try to do too much or do nothing at all. Remember, you are starting year after year traditions.

Step #5: Be flexible

- Anticipate the unexpected. Respond to what happens spontaneously.
- Avoid guilt. When it doesn't go as well or as often as you expected, resist being disappointed.
- Let these traditions grow and develop over the years. Guard the core purpose of your traditions but adapt them to the changing age, energy, personality and circumstances of your growing family.

John Lewis is a father of three grown children and husband of one Christmas-loving wife. He is the director of Kingdom Story and passionate about seeing the next generation of Jesus followers grow and stay faithful over their life time. May your kids, year after year, grow to anticipate the faith element of Christmas alongside all the fun of the season!

Advent Can Be a Quiet Adventure

by Jody Collins

Have you ever had to move houses during the Christmas season? No? Well, allow me to tell you a story. Twenty-five years ago, our family journeyed from California to Seattle during the holidays and I discovered something.

In the middle of a living room crowded with moving boxes, I had to surrender my ideas of what Christmas "should" look like, leaving space for God to surprise our family beyond what we could imagine. I was forced to adjust to a new season as I viewed things, not as I dreamed they would be, but the way they were.

My ideas of what-was-to-come, a new home, settling in, making it my own—had kept me going through those few months. But oddly enough, as I looked around at our temporary rental with its empty walls and barely furnished rooms, my mental state greatly improved. It made it easier to 'see' the future. Why? Because although I felt untethered and impatient, desperate to begin nesting in our new home, the emptiness created room for waiting.

The focus and intent of the Advent season is just that, providing space to wait—physically, spiritually and mentally—to celebrate the birth of Christ.

My faith background is tempered by an Evangelical perspective, so Advent and all it represents is new to me. I love the slowing down that the Sunday candle lighting affords my husband and I, along with its focus on Christ's presence, not the day of All the Presents.

As a newcomer to this observance, I was surprised to learn that Advent was originally a period of fasting in preparation for the feast of the Nativity (now Christmas) and practiced in some form as early as 400 AD. Unfortunately for us, Advent as a season of fasting and reflection has all but disappeared from many church landscapes. It has been defined, instead, as the number of shopping/party/activity days there are until Christmas, and thus, we have gift-driven Advent 'calendars.' These are, actually, December calendars, not Advent calendars.

The practice of fasting seems like a shocking suggestion prior to the rich celebration of Christmas, but it makes sense when you think about it. Letting go, putting off or making room for one thing, makes space for something else.

Like the empty walls in our new rental house all those years ago, extra space can help us "see" better without all the distractions. When the too much of Christmas presses in, it helps to make room for the joy we crave by saying "no" to what we don't need.

Instead of the usual going without food, fasting during Advent can simply be a variation of giving up, putting off, setting aside or laying down. All these provide a way to make room for Jesus in our soul and spirit, where we are hungriest. Because, goodness knows, there are scores of things that want to "feed" us; too much of anything can fill me so full that I never know I'm hungry. Fasting is one way to make room for God to show up, and hunger can often provide a way for us to say no to our overstuffed senses.

But fasting doesn't have to be just from food.

How About Fasting from Noise?

Turn off your screens—phones, tablets, computers—for sixty to ninety minutes and relish the freedom that quiet brings. Of course, it may be noisy now that you've got time to read one more book to your kids. But that's a good kind of noise, the kind that feeds the soul— their's and your's. Having young children and teens limit their visual media input is a way they can also fast. You might say, "Sometimes there's noise we hear and sometimes there's noise we see. All that makes it hard to hear and see God. Mom and Dad are going to spend less time with their phone/computer/tablet during Advent. When would you like to give up some of your screen time?" This phrasing frames the question in a way that communicates they will cut back, but it also gives them the power of making the choice of how and when.

I'm not talking about stopping all visual media but taking baby steps to help children adjust their thinking, too. The point is to make room for God to speak to us in that still, small voice; He will show up in the space that we give Him. That's what Advent is all about– preparing room for the Saviour to come.

Fast from the "Shoulds"

The overwhelming amount of Christmas trappings even at the grocery store can be hard to ignore—everyone has to eat, and thus we are inundated with the visual overload of the holidays. It's hard to ignore. "Decorate like this! Buy this! Your home should look like this!" It feels like the displays are shouting from the aisles.

We can't forego feeding our families, but we can take an intentional break during the Christmas season from visual media channels that keep us focused on all those 'shoulds.' Facebook's siren song or Pinterest and Instagram come to mind—whatever social vortex seems to suck you in. These platforms can be helpful for creativity but can also be a rabbit hole of, "Oooohhh, I should make this. No, I should try this." Lay it down. Turn it off. Put it away.

Fasting from Food

Of course, your children will need their three squares a day. Growing children need fuel to stay well, keep growing, and continue learning . . . and to be happy. The practice of fasting from food when it comes to your kids is clearly fraught with questions. Should they participate? Will they even understand what they're doing? What's the point?

Consider this. If our children get everything they want whenever they want it, we all know this is not a good thing. One way to help children understand they cannot always have whatever they want is to practice even a simple fast.

What about fasting from certain foods as a family? Saving your enjoyment for Christmas when you will break your fast together? Perhaps meats—ham, beef, whatever—sweets or a particular treat. Or, you could set aside Sundays, traditionally "feast days" on the church calendar, as days to look forward to those special foods. (Chocolate totally counts.) My friend, Kay, says she and her family fast from sugar during the week and mark Sunday as the day to indulge.

Setting aside one day as different is another way to simply mark the time as special.

Fasting during the holidays doesn't have to be cold-turkey (sorry), but more of a subtle shift in thinking about the way we look at Christmas with all its too much. Consider taking out all the fake "food" that promises to feed our soul and replacing it with holy nutrition.

Honoring, adopting or adapting one of the earliest traditions of Advent is a simple way to make room for more joy and peace this Christmas season. And the best news? There's nothing you need to add to your busy life, but something to take away. Literally.

Sometimes the best "yes" is a "no". What a simple yet powerful gift.[7]

Jody Collins is a faith writer and poetry lover living in the Pacific Northwest with her very patient husband. She's been penning words since Smith-Corona typewriters graced the desks of her middle school, but nowadays you can find her at www.jodyleecollins.com. Connect on Instagram or Facebook where she posts way too many photos of her six grandchildren.

Taking Time for Joy

by Lilly Lewin

With all that is going on globally, I need the reminder that Joy does exist and I need to actually PRACTICE finding joy in my daily life. Sometimes it's hard to describe how we find Joy. So it helps to think of the opposite of Joy.

I think it also helps to identify what takes away our joy. What things pop right into your head when I ask, *What steals your joy?* For me, it's things like traffic, too much noise, too much TV (especially news), lack of sleep, and paperwork!

So for Advent, I need to plan ways to avoid these things. And to notice when these and other things are stealing my joy! What are your Joy Stealers? And how can we plan ways to avoid Joy Stealers this holiday season?

Step 1: Identify your Joy Stealers. Make a list!

Step 2: Make a plan and choose to lose the Joy Stealing actions and activities in the days ahead!

Step 3: Identify what brings you Joy and start practicing these things!

Step 4: Start watching for Joy! Notice when Joy happens! Document JOY sightings!

Where do you find Joy? What things naturally bring JOY to you?

I find JOY in hanging out with children. Their curiosity and sense of wonder remind me that I need to be more curious and more wonder seeking! A few years ago, I spent some time in a third-grade classroom and even though it was late afternoon, they were still curious and still saw things I wouldn't normally see. We were talking about why the trees lose their leaves in the Fall and about photosynthesis and one boy noticed that a leaf seemed to be hanging off the tree all on its own, no branch in site! It was hanging by a spider web thread being gently blown by the wind. That's the gift of noticing! Finding joy in the small things and taking time to notice them!

Which leads me to a second way I find JOY: being out in nature. What things in nature bring you JOY? Watching sunsets are one of my favorite joy sources! The Fall colors bring me joy, too. And I absolutely love snow! Maybe watching a squirrel climb a tree or your cat investigate your briefcase or shopping bag can bring you joy and make you smile. Maybe plan some outdoor adventure or cook some s'mores over a fire pit. Take time to notice the beauty of Creation and take time to be thankful.

If you have children at home or friends with kids, take time to ask them what makes them smile and this can help you catch Joy too! Volunteer in a classroom or take a walk with a child and notice what they notice, like the leaves, the bugs, the faces and shapes in the clouds.

Maybe you find joy when you take time to create something. It could be baking something or making something with your hands. Perhaps you could choose to turn off the TV or step away from the computer or phone and make or do something that brings you joy. Dust off your bicycle or get your sled to get ready for that first snow fall. Shoot hoops, swing on a swing, or plant something. Make a new playlist with songs that bring joy to your heart and a smile to your face and listen to them regularly. Share that playlist with a friend to pass along the JOY! I love baking chocolate chip cookies and pumpkin muffins from scratch. The process of baking is joy-filled. And giving them to my neighbors adds to that joy.

What about you? What are your Joy Sightings? As a practice for Advent, take time to notice the things that bring a smile to your face. Document Joy Sightings! Write them down or take a picture with your phone to help you remember. We could even start a hashtag for Advent and share these joy-filled things with each other to help spread the JOY to the world.

Please join me in Joy and #Joysighting this Advent!

Lilly is a worship curator, speaker, author, artist, and founder of thinplaceNASHVILLE, and freerangeworship.com She creates sacred space prayer experiences and leads workshops & retreats across the country and beyond. She writes the freerangefriday blog each week at Godspacelight.com

Pray, Plan, Prepare, Practice

by Christine Sine

Just before Advent, I often facilitate a small contemplative retreat day at our home in Seattle. I always enjoy preparing for these days which gives me an important opportunity to relax and refresh myself, too. They remind me of the preparation I need to do to get myself ready for a new season and encourage me to create new practices for my own spiritual life.

The focus is on developing a rhythm of life for the Advent season and beyond. I encourage participants to create their own unique rhythm based on a process of prayer, planning, preparation and practice. I talk about the violence we do to our souls by succumbing to the rush and pressure of modern life and Parker Palmer's assertion that we need to know when and where to seek sanctuary for our souls. If we don't have a place that provides sanctuary, our lives spin out of control and our rhythm becomes distorted.

This is where we need prayer:

Prayer

The prayer that draws us into the place of sanctuary isn't what most of us think about when we imagine prayer. Once I would have been happy to see the waiting season of Advent as a time to pray according to the prescribed patterns the lectionary calls us to, but not anymore. Nor do the traditional symbols of Advent wreaths and Christmas music any longer provide sanctuary for my soul. These are the forms of prayer and practice prescribed by a culture hundreds of years ago.

Now I need something new, something that encourages me to wait by reaching deep into the depths of my soul and look for something that resonates with who God has created me to be. This is a prayer that begins in silence, a prayer that draws me deep into my inner being, into what Parker Palmer calls "the place of not-knowing", that beckons us all to relax and slow down, often in the darkness, "until our eyes adjust and we start to see what's down there." As Palmer says, "I want

49

to make my own discoveries, think my own thoughts and feel my own feelings before I learn what the experts say."[8]

It often takes darkness to enable us to think for ourselves and experiment with something new. We learn not to hurry what God is doing or try to force a pathway that is not divinely inspired. Out of this kind of prayer comes a plan and a rhythm that is uniquely our own, a rhythm that is easier to stick with because it has risen from the depths of our souls.

What are the prayers that lie in the dark and wait to bubble up from inside your soul as you prepare for the Advent and Christmas season?

Planning

Another of my favorite authors, Christine Valters Paintner, comments in her latest book, *The Soul's Slow Ripening*, that, "the soul thrives in slowness and that the divine spark of life reveals itself when we simply pay attention."[9] Paying attention to the prayers that have been birthed, rooted and now grow in the dark, in the slow place of contemplation, experimentation and discovery, often results in unexpected but important plans that can form the firm foundations we need for our seasonal rhythms.

Waiting in the silence, growing in the dark, allowing roots to find anchor in the soil, this is the kind of planning that has invited me to unleash my creativity and develop new practices.

In what ways are you paying attention to the divine spark within you, promoting you to slow down and take notice?

Preparing

There are three things that help me prepare for a new season:

- Going on retreat[10] — as many of you know, this is something that Tom and I do three or four times a year. It is an extremely important part of my preparation for any new season.
- Consult a soul friend[11] – the soul friend or *Anam Cara* was "a person to whom you could reveal the hidden intimacies of your life".[12] O'Donohue goes on to say, "A friend is a loved one who awakens your life in order to free the wild possibilities within you".[13] Isn't that beautiful? I am privileged to have several good friends who provide soul friendship for me, some of whom have

done so for decades. It is part of what has given my faith resilience through the tough times I have passed through.

- Plan some fun — it is only in the last few years, and particularly as I worked on *The Gift of Wonder,* that I came to believe in a God who loves fun, laughs frequently and delights in me and whom I am created to be. According to play expert Dr. Stuart Brown, "nothing lights up the brain like play". He believes that play might be God's greatest gift to humankind. Nurturing my relationship with this fun-loving God has refreshed my soul and has given me permission to enjoy life in every season.

What steps are you taking to prepare for the upcoming season?

Practicing

Out of this framework of preparation comes the new practices that I engage in. A couple of years ago, it was the fun activity of creating an Advent Jar[14] that really helped me focus and develop a sustainable rhythm for the season of Advent. It was my first experience with spray painting a jar — something I have wanted to do for a long time. The following year, I spray painted a whole collection of small terra cotta pots which formed my Advent calendar. I had a ball, both in the preparation and in the anticipation of my upcoming practice for the new season.

What new practice resonates in your soul as you get ready for Advent?

Christine describes herself as a contemplative activist, passionate gardener, author, and liturgist. She is the founder of Godspace and her most recent book is The Gift of Wonder: Creative Practices for Delighting in God.

Week 1 of Advent: Waiting in Silence

A Scottish Blessing for Advent

May the blessing of Light be on you
Light without and light within,
May the blessed sunlight shine on you
And warm your heart till it glows like
A great peat fire, so that the stranger
May come and warm himself at it,
And also a friend.
And may the light shine out of the two eyes of you,
Like a candle set in two windows of a house,
Bidding the wanderer to come in out of the storm.

And may the blessing of the Rain be on you
The soft sweet rain. May it fall upon your spirit
So that all the little flowers may spring up,
And shed their sweetness on the air.
And may the blessing of the Great Rains be on
You, may they beat upon your spirit
And wash it fair and clean,
And leave there many a shining pool
Where the blue of heaven shines,
And sometimes a star.

And may the blessing of the Earth be on you
The great round earth; may you ever have
A kindly greeting for them you pass
As you're going along the roads.

May the earth be soft under you when you rest upon it,
Tired at the end of the day,
And may it rest easy over you when,
At the last, you lay out under it;
May it rest so lightly over you,
That your soul may be out from under it quickly,
And up, and off, and on its way to God.

(Scottish Blessing, source known[15], copyright unknown)

First Week of Advent

by Lilly Lewin

This week, we light the first candle in our Advent wreaths. The first candle is known as the **HOPE** candle or the **PROPHET** Candle depending upon what flavor of church you grew up in.

I am very grateful that **HOPE** is the first candle because I am in need of **HOPE** this week and this year.

HOPE for healing for friends who are hurting both physically and emotionally.

HOPE for our world that is broken and bleeding with wars and famine.

HOPE for refugees around the world who just want a safe place to live.

HOPE for those who are living in fear and want to build walls rather than bridges.

And I'm grateful for the **HOPE** that the Prophets gave the Children of Israel and give to each of us today!

Isaiah 9:2 (NLT) reminds us that, "The people walking in darkness have seen a great light; on those living in the land of deep darkness a light has dawned."

The Prophet Jeremiah reminds us:

> The days are surely coming, says the Lord, when I will fulfill the promise I made to the house of Israel and the house of Judah. In those days and at that time I will cause a righteous Branch to spring up for David; and he shall execute justice and righteousness in the land. In those days Judah will be saved and Jerusalem will live in safety. And this is the name by which it will be called: 'The Lord is our righteousness' (Jeremiah 33:14-16 NRSV).

What hope do you need today? What things give you hope?

56

What things help you have hope on dark days? A sunrise? A baby's smile? A great cup of coffee in the morning? Make a list and refer to it often. Take time to find a bit of Hope each day.

How can you plan to see more light this Advent, rather than dwelling in the darkness? What adds LIGHT to your life? What can you do to bring LIGHT to your world, your family, your neighbors? Start by lighting an actual candle.

What righteousness and justice would you like to see Jesus execute in your land, your life, your neighborhood? Set a timer on your phone and pray daily for a place or an area that needs the justice of Jesus and the healing of his righteousness. Find a globe ornament, add it to your tree to remind you to pray for places around the world that need justice, healing, and hope.

Here's one of my favorite prayers to pray during Advent.

Lord God,
Calm us as we wait for the Gift of Jesus
Cleanse us to prepare the way for his arrival.
Help us to slow down and prepare our hearts.
Help us to wait and take time to be with you.
Teach us to contemplate the wonder of God with us.
Teach us to know the presence of your Spirit.
Teach us to bear the life of Jesus and live out his Kingdom.
Today and Always.
Amen[16]

May we all feel the Hope of Jesus this Advent and may we all shine his Light and be bearers of Hope to our world.

Lilly is a worship curator, speaker, author, artist, and founder of thinplaceNASHVILLE, and freerangeworship.com She creates sacred space prayer experiences and leads workshops & retreats across the country and beyond. She writes the freerangefriday blog each week at Godspacelight.com

Stilling our Souls in a Chaotic World

by Joy Lenton

Resting isn't just about stepping down or drawing back from chaotic busyness and the things which distract us from nurturing our soul life, it's also about coming into a still, calm place where we can listen better to what God is doing in our lives and in the world. It involves a conscious tuning out in order to fully tune in to his voice.

One day, I was becoming anxious about my persistent ill health preventing me from fulfilling what I saw as the calling on my life. Dropping deep into my ingratitude and frustration, I sensed God whispering these words: *"Sitting at the feet of Jesus is your calling. Everything else will flow from it."*

Wow, I thought, how deceptively simple yet profound! Here is a calling for every Christian believer. Above any other thing, we are all called to give Jesus the pre-eminence he deserves in our lives, and that's hard to do when we're overly stretched.

Then I wondered: What might sitting at Jesus' feet look like? Something like this, perhaps…

- an attitude of humility, reverence, submission
- recognition of his Lordship over all things
- a soul's prompt, obedient surrender
- a willingness to listen and learn
- a heart's devotion, worship and praise
- a receptive mind yielding to God's word
- a soul at rest and peace, in harmony, complete

There is great value in stillness, after all. "Stillness is what gives stability. And it is what keeps the wheels falling off our lives".[17]

The story of Mary and Martha (Lk 10:38-42) always speaks to me. We witness Martha willingly opening her home to Jesus, though her heart was diverted away from being as receptive and attentive to his teaching as her sister, Mary, was because she allowed extra busyness to distract her from achieving inner stillness.

What had Jesus come for? I think he wanted the solace of their friendship as his darkest hour drew nigh. Maybe he was not so much hungry for food and drink as for soul company, for someone to drink in his words, listen to their meaning and find their inner thirst satiated in him.

Mary saw into his soul and answered its cry for a soul companion, while Martha saw the lean fatigue in his face and answered with food. Sadly, her distractedness caused anger and resentment to build up. Martha experienced that inner tug-of-war we all feel at times between duty and devotion.

Our souls long for peaceful contemplation and restful quietude. We scorn the need, drown it out with activities which are not necessarily wrong in themselves but which take us away from what our souls crave most. Our inner voice is always urging us toward rest and peace, and we so often ignore its gentle persuasion.

Fear of missing out, fear of being still, fear of what we'll hear when we stop—all of these and more will hold us back from moving in that direction. Although we really do need sacred spaces in our days, because a stilled soul is an alert and receptive soul into which God will pour wisdom and instruction.

As I read the biblical account of Mary and Martha, I can easily relate to Martha, because my default mode used to be fussing and fretting when wanting to organise things. However, decades of being chronically sick with M.E have altered that trait somewhat. I've grown used to not being a physically strong, active, outwardly busy person and more drawn toward a contemplative frame of mind.

I actually need to be still, pace, and take enforced rest on a daily basis because it's best for me. But we don't have to wait until sickness derails us in order to appreciate the benefits of stilling our body and soul before God, because you and I can quit the chaos whenever we decide to come quietly before him. There is abundant joy, peace and solace to be found in his presence. *What greater incentive do we need?*

Joy Lenton is a contemplative Christian writer from Norfolk, England, who suffers from M.E and multiple chronic illness. Her writing and books assist others to sense the sacred in the everyday and discover hope in painful and challenging circumstances. She would love to connect with you at her Poetry Joy and Words of Joy blogs or on Facebook.

Into the Whirlwind

by Andy Wade

Help! I'm drowning! That's how I often feel this time of year. It's not just preparing for Advent and Christmas that gets me stressed. For several years I co-ordinated the warming shelter in Hood River Oregon. I was always gearing up to open our warming shelter for the season. Scrambling to find a location for the shelter, training new volunteers, preparing posters, flyers, and essential shelter documents… the list goes on and on.

Don't get me wrong, I enjoyed volunteering for the shelter. I found great wisdom and compassion in my friends living outside as well as the team tasked with putting it all together.

I am currently facilitator for M25 the Gorge focusing on immigrant/immigration issues and walking with our Latinx neighbors. I'm also serving on the Gorge Ecumenical Ministries board and I still face the same kinds of pressures.

Every year October and November seem to collide like the perfect storm. It's like the year speeds up from both ends and smashes together with a thunderous clash. My heart races, my stress level elevates, and anxiety seeps in through the fissures. I sometimes feel like the disciples must have felt on that boat in the middle of a tumultuous lake:

> One day Jesus said to his disciples, "Let's cross to the other side of the lake." So they got into a boat and started out. As they sailed across, Jesus settled down for a nap. But soon a fierce storm came down on the lake. The boat was filling with water, and they were in real danger.
> The disciples went and woke him up, shouting, "Master, Master, we're going to drown! When Jesus woke up, he rebuked the wind and the raging waves. Suddenly the storm stopped and all was calm. Then he asked them, "Where is your faith?" The disciples were terrified and amazed. "Who is this man?" they asked each other. "When he gives a command, even the wind and waves obey him!" (Lk 8:22-15 NLT).

OK, yes, I sometimes feel like Jesus is asleep at the helm. I can admit that. I can also recognize his voice asking me, *Where is your faith?* I know God has called me to be the facilitator for M25 the Gorge and serve on the Gorge Ecumenical Ministries board. I've gotten into that boat. The questions I'm left with are:

- How do I push through the storms with courage and faith?
- Where can I find calm and shelter during the storms?

The Right Boat

First and foremost, I must ask if I'm doing things I'm not supposed to be doing. Have I gotten into the wrong boat? That's a difficult question that takes discernment from those close to us who understand what we've taken on and why.

The problem often isn't that we're doing bad things, rather that we've taken on projects, parties, tasks, or responsibilities (you fill in the blanks) that are not right for this season in our lives. Take time to evaluate your current and potential commitments. How do they line up with your sense of God's tug on your life right now? Do you have a small group or someone you can go to who can confirm these choices?

The Right Crew

Now that I'm focused on the things I'm supposed to be doing, what does my support network look like? I need people around me who can encourage, pray, and listen well to my rants and complaints when times get tough. For me that means a small group from church and a couple of close friends. Who is giving you support?

The Right Shelters

I also need times to just get away. To be honest, I don't do a good job scheduling these times into my life. I would have better balance if I did. I do have a pretty good internal mechanism that lets me know when my emotions and energy are getting out of sync. That's often when I call my brother and suggest it's time for another mushroom hunt, camping trip, or both!

I'm refreshed by the wilderness and filled with wonder at God's diverse creation. I just returned from one such campout and, even though it poured rain half the time we were out, I feel renewed. Where do you find renewal, refreshment, and energy? How can you be more deliberate about regularly scheduling those things into your routine during this holiday season?

The Right Captain

Out in that boat, far from shore, the disciples had a crisis. It happens. As we cross through the waters of Advent and Christmas, we may well experience our own crisis. When the disciples cried out to Jesus, he was only feet away, resting in the stern of the boat.

This reminds me that I need to stay close to Jesus. What that means may look different for each one of us, but we need to ask ourselves, what makes me feel close to God? We might also want to ask ourselves, what makes me feel distant from God?

These two questions frame for us our spiritual temperament. Knowing the answers to these two questions will help us to incorporate more of what draws us closer to God while eliminating those things that draw us away from God. If we want to be guided and reassured by God's presence, then we need to make sure that God is in the boat with us.

The Right Attitude

Chaos will come. We can do what we can to cut personal chaos out of our lives and get control over our own busyness, but this time of year, the world is amped up. Recognizing this helps us to reframe the season, to recognize the wind is howling, but know that we don't have to get caught up in the storm. This kind of honesty protects us from anger, frustration, and anxiety. With this bit of inner peace, walking back through the points I've suggested becomes much easier.

- How are you feeling about the coming seasons of Advent and Christmas and all that comes with them?
- What boat are you in? Is it the right boat?
- Who is your crew? Who are you crewing for?
- Have you identified your shelters along the way? What are they?
- How close are you to the Captain? Are there things you can put into place now that will draw you close and keep you closer?

Andy Wade is the facilitator for M25 the Gorge focusing on immigrant/ immigration issues and walking with our Latinx neighbors. He serves on the Gorge Ecumenical Ministries board and lives in Hood River, OR with his wife, Susan.

Waiting to Exhale

by Cynthia Helton

Resting in chaos is meant to help us all focus on better preparing ourselves for the celebration of the coming of Christ – rather than becoming bogged down in the minutia of the usual materialistic, consumer-driven hype the holidays have become.

But unfortunately, that net has widened over the last week to push chaos to an all-new level, incorporating the dismay, the disillusionment, the distress of our political climate here in the US to a level that far surpasses the normal angst of the season.

Dark days (and nights) of the soul on display for all the world to see. So much so that the hustle and bustle of holiday mania may quite literally be the proverbial straw that broke the camel's back. Perhaps we all need a ledge to stand on; we need to get our perspective back. Perhaps we need this "wilderness" just as Jesus did to bring into focus the opportunity for transformation that is germinating in these shadows.

Perhaps resting in chaos doesn't necessarily mean getting "rid" of chaos; but rather being still long enough to absorb the fact that what happens to one of us happens to all of us in some way, shape or fashion.

I've often wondered, did the "human" Jesus completely understand what was happening within him after his baptism in the Jordan by John the Baptist? Did he have an inkling that something was about to happen — to him and because of him? Did he wonder if his path was due to his own understanding… Or did he always know he was God?

Some may totally disagree with me, and since I'm certainly no scholar or trained clergy, my thoughts are my own; but it gives me a modicum of comfort to think Jesus was "fully" human, and perhaps his own divinity was revealed to him slowly, over the course of his life. Like with the rest of us.

I read recently that, "Christ" wasn't Jesus' last name! Christ came after the resurrection. The Jesus we first meet as the innocent child gave up his outward divinity in order to show us our own "inward" divinity. Jesus was preparing — consciously or unconsciously — to welcome the Christ he would be for all eternity.

So what am I getting at? I'm suggesting that this chaos we're finding ourselves in… be it personal, financial, political, or all of the above… can be our "gift". Rather than trying to deny it exists, deny we're possibly a "holy mess", let us use this unsettling time to our advantage.

Like Jesus in the wilderness, let us see our demons for what they are: our fears… feeling disconnected from God… searching for what we think we've lost. Let us use this time to reflect on the fact that the incarnate Christ really comes to us over-and-over again, like the ebb and flow of our lives… a continual Advent. Actually, that makes me feel hopeful.

When Christmas Day comes and we celebrate the birth of human Jesus who is the Christ, we get a glimpse of what love looks like. The outpouring of the Divine is incarnate in our midst. We are filled personally, and that spills out into the world. I think trying to hold on to that feeling — for everything to be perfect — is what happens to many of us. It's how we get caught up in this seasonal "frenzy" that consumes us, leaving us depressed and exhausted.

Is it possible that we can look at this chaos in a different way — choosing to see a blessing it can hold if we call it by its right name? Maybe cleansing or polishing? Or, how about tilling the soil or pruning? All of these words connote more than work, and effort, and frustration — like wandering in the desert… but look at our treasure in store for us when we "exhale".

Cynthia is a Voyager in the Community of Aidan and Hilda (CA&H), a dispersed ecumenical community of members committed to living a Way of Life in the Christian Celtic tradition. She lives in North Texas, just south of Dallas, with her husband of thirty-three years.

The Whisper of Christmas

by Talitha Fraser

Decorations are in stores and carols are on repeat, the crackers seem to show up right after Halloween. For some, this is a time of year when you can feel a lot of pressure — things to finish off before the end of the year, things to plan, presents to buy, cards to write, people to see, family visiting or visiting family. Rather than a list of things to do, how can we tune in to what Christmas is really about, how can we listen for the whisper of Christmas?

Baking or any other craft at this time of year can be a gift in more ways than one. There is something soothing to be found in following basic instructions, getting your hands dirty, feeling like you are making something with tangible evidence of results from your work.

It's tempting to want to retreat from everything, get away from the commercialization and the crowds, and family responsibilities, then my Christmas could be "holy". But then I'm also running away from the lesson of Incarnation, the enfleshing of God — the lesson that we who are followers of Jesus don't run from the secular stuff; but rather we try to transform it.

In his book, *The Whisper of Christmas*, Joe Pennel, Jr. tells us:

> There is no evidence of any kind regarding the date of Jesus' birth. His nativity began to be celebrated on Dec. 25 in Rome during the early part of the fourth century (336 AD) as a Christian counterpart to the pagan festival, popular among the worshipers of Mithras, called Sol Invictus, the Unconquerable Sun. At the very moment when the days are the shortest and darkness seems to have conquered light, the sun passes its nadir. Days grow longer, and although the cold will only increase for quite a long time, the ultimate conquest of winter is sure. This astronomical process is a parable of the career of the Incarnate One. At the moment when history is blackest, and in the least expected and obvious place, the Son of God is born…[18]

So the secular speaks to the sacred, and sacred to the secular. I encourage you to bake or make something, there are some suggestions below, and you might like to invite others to share in it with you or make them as gifts. Take something in your hands, be present, and find something sustaining in something simple and homemade. What is evoked by these smells of ginger, cinnamon, vanilla, chocolate…?

Take a moment to sit in silence, however you feel comfortable, and just "be". Slow your breathing… let everything that's in your head, everything going on, rise up and then let it go… I invite you to be open to the advent of God.

Try to recapture and be present to some of the wonder, mystery, and believing in fragile miracles that can make this time of year meaningful and transforming for us as followers of Christ and believers in hope and love born out of darkness.

Bula, Afio mai, Wominjeka, Haere mai… Welcome our God of wonder…

For some making and baking suggestions, check out the resources at the end of this devotional.

Talitha is a Kiwi urban contemplative theopoetics-dabbler living in Melbourne, Australia. With a strong calling toward encountering God and creating spaces where others may also, she seeks to live out this out bivocationally living in intentional community. Her poems and reflections can be found at itellyouarise and thelightanddarkofit.

Being Still Amid the Christmas Rush

by Rev. Jeannie Kendall

One day this summer, I was waiting to speak to one of our volunteer receptionists, but it was clear there would be a slight delay. Unthinkingly, I said, "I'll just take my cleaning in" — a two-minute job I could do anytime. "You are like me," she said. "You can't sit still". I simply smiled.

Later that week, I took a walk in a local small nature reserve. Tucked among the houses, it's a small urban wilderness awash with birdsong: somewhere you can be almost guaranteed a rare moment of isolation.

As I meandered through the twisting pathways, several times there flitted across my path a brightly coloured butterfly. Yellow-green and vibrant, I wanted to capture its image, partly to identify it, and partly, even allowing for the limitations of a photograph, to depict its beauty. In the event, it would not allow me to do either. It refused to stop, moving ceaselessly and not stopping even for a moment for the summer sunshine to catch its wings.

Seeking to see more closely the birds darting across a clearing, I sat for a moment on an old, fallen, tree, once alive but now stripped of bark yet still beautiful in its exposed vulnerability. The birds remained elusive, yet, as I persevered, a peacock butterfly came and gently rested on the bare wood. In contrast to its restless distant relative, it seemed unhurried, and I was able to appreciate its extraordinary markings and even to capture the moment, however, inadequately.

I have only recently begun to realise that, yes, I'm not good at sitting still, unless the inactivity has another purpose, such as writing or listening to someone. I would imagine that (like most things) it is a mixture of the way I am wired and circumstance. Certainly growing up in a hospital, (where my father worked and so, because of its remote setting, we were obliged to live there) I was unusually aware from an early age of the fragility of life and its brevity. So packing plenty into each day somehow became inured.

Our ceaseless activity can, of course, have many geneses with varying degrees of health, from a profoundly anxious restlessness to the uninhibited and joyous grasping of the moment that we see in children.

This time of year brings for many of us a restless overactivity. Some is necessary, but perhaps it is a good moment to pause and consider — might something other than necessity be driving it? Are we searching for some perfect Christmas which exists only in fiction and not in the reality of our lives? Are we afraid to lose love from people around us if we do not get it right? What makes it so difficult to simply pause, regroup, and take a moment to be still and silent?

Jesus understood our difficulty. Those of us who may find it difficult to linger in the moment need, I suspect, to regularly hear again his word to agitated disciples: "Come to me. Get away with me and you'll recover your life. I'll show you how to take a real rest. Walk with me and work with me—watch how I do it. Learn the unforced rhythms of grace. Keep company with me and you'll learn to live freely and lightly." (Matthew 11:28-30 The Message).

The unforced rhythms of grace are very, very different from our own, and profoundly countercultural. Few, perhaps, really achieve living like that. The peacock butterfly though, ah yes, my tree-sharing friend had grasped what I so often fail to, and I was richer for it. This season I want not to lose the lesson of that balmy summer day.

My prayer for myself and those of you who read this, is that somehow this advent and Christmas we hold on to some moments of stillness and, when we have lost them, to at least look within to wonder why.

Jeannie Kendall works freelance writing and teaching. She lives in Surrey with her husband and has two grown up children and two grandchildren. Her first book, Finding Our Voice, was published by Authentic Media in 2019 and her second, on the subject of tears, is due out in 2021. Her website is www.jeanniekendall.co.uk

Is Joseph the Unsung Hero of the Advent Story?

by Christine Sine

At the beginning of Advent, I set up my sacred space specially for Advent. I get out my icon of the Annunciation and my beautiful photo of the Magnificat stained glass window at the Taizé community in France. Then I work on my Advent garden. As I worked on this, I realized that there was still something, or should I say someone, missing from my display — Joseph.

So I went looking for images of Joseph with a pregnant Mary. They are hard to find, unless I want Christmas card images of them heading towards Bethlehem. One of the best is from the Catholic Cathedral in Wichita, Kansas, a beautiful sculpture by Rip Caswell[19] that holds me enthralled whenever I look at it. The sculpture shows Joseph standing behind and embracing a very pregnant Mary with an expression of love on his face. I love the sense of protection and caring this sculpture conveys. Joseph must have been an extraordinary man, yet we rarely think about how loving his behavior was towards Mary.

According to New Testament theologian Kenneth Bailey, we misinterpret Matthew 1:20, "As he considered this, an angel of the Lord appeared to him in a dream. 'Joseph, son of David,' the angel said, 'do not be afraid to take Mary as your wife. For the child within her was conceived by the Holy Spirit'." He says, "'he considered this' should be translated 'he became angry' and planned not to marry her."[20] Not an unexpected reaction for a righteous man who finds his betrothed is pregnant by another 'man'.

The amazing thing is that Joseph changed his mind because of a dream. How easily he could have ignored the angel. His acceptance of Mary and the baby she carried had consequences not just for her reputation, but for his, too. From the viewpoint of those around, either the child was his and he was not quite as just and righteous as they previously thought, or the child was someone else's and he was a fool to accept Mary. He would have been" just" in condoning her stoning. Yet he stood by her. What courage it must have taken to stand against the culture of his day.

I love the way that Kenneth Bailey talks about Joseph in his wonderful book, *Jesus Through Middle Eastern Eyes*.

> "In his cameo appearance, Matthew presents Joseph as a human being of remarkable spiritual stature. He possessed the boldness, daring, courage and strength of character to stand up against his entire community and take Mary as his wife. He did so in spite of the forces that no doubt wanted her stoned. His vision of justice stayed his hand. In short, he was able to reprocess his anger into grace."[21]

That Joseph's extraordinary love protected and surrounded Mary and eventually Jesus continues to be seen as the story unfolds. Bailey suggests that Joseph took Mary to Bethlehem because he was unsure what would happen to her if he left her in Nazareth[22]. His willingness to flee with her into Egypt and his teaching of Jesus to be a carpenter are also indications of his love and care.

What Is Your Response?

Take a few minutes to contemplate the Rip Carwell's sculpture. Pay particular attention to Joseph standing behind Mary. Imagine Joseph as a courageous and loving man, supporting Mary by standing against the law of his culture. What are your thoughts as you gaze on this image? How does it change your impression of Joseph and his place in the story of Jesus?

Now take a few minutes to think about your own father. Some of us have loving fathers and it is not hard for us to imagine them standing in support of our mothers when they were pregnant with us. Others have less loving impressions. The abuse and violence of my own father meant that I ignored Joseph for a long time. I also ignored the loving gestures my father made towards me. When I was a premature infant in the baby incubator, it was my father who brought the milk my mother expressed to the hospital each day. It was my father who provided a home and food. As I look at this image, I can imagine his love for me and my mother, even though he was rarely able to express it.

Who else has been a father to you? For those of us who don't have loving fathers to look back at, God often provides substitutes, loving friends or relatives who take the place of fathers and help us create healthy images of a father's love. I suspect that Joseph did this for Jesus. The stories of his conception by the power of the Holy Spirit must have created distant father images for Jesus, extraordinary as his knowledge of God was. Was it Joseph who formed early impressions of a God of love for Jesus before he fully understood who he was? Was it Joseph who provided loving images that made it possible for him to call God, "Abba", and share stories of the warm welcome for prodigal sons? Obviously, we do not know but it warms my heart to think of these possibilities.

Christine describes herself as a contemplative activist, passionate gardener, author, and liturgist. She is the founder of Godspace and her most recent book is The Gift of Wonder: Creative Practices for Delighting in God.

Week 2 of Advent: Waiting for a Vulnerable God

Echoes of Advent

by Andy Wade

I wrote this poem after a couple of weeks of reflecting on these changes of church seasons. Advent to Christmas to Epiphany and on. The promise began long ago, announced its arrival in Mary's song, and burst into the world surrounded by animals. But that was not the end of the story.

Almost unnoticed,
A glow in the distance
Beckoning hope
Compels me forward

Comfort the people
My heart whimpers
Only half believing
This light will matter

Mary's song fills the air
Relief for the orphan
Release for the captive
Jubilee

A baby cries out
Welcomed by outcasts
Visited by foreigners
Threatened by empire

Down to Egypt
And back again
A familiar journey
For slave and trader

Rejected
Mocked
Tortured
Buried

Flickering for a moment
Then bursting back to life
Advent echoes
Throughout history

Andy Wade is the facilitator for M25 the Gorge focusing on immigrant/immigration issues and walking with our Latinx neighbors. He serves on the Gorge Ecumenical Ministries board and lives in Hood River, OR with his wife, Susan.

Entering the World with Jesus

by Joy Lenton

On Advent Sunday, as we ready ourselves to remember the infant-birth arrival on earth of our Lord and Saviour, the first candle is lit on an Advent wreath as an emblem of our faith. It's a sign offering hope to all, while they make their way through this world's darkness, and a glowing reminder of the luminous Light of Christ in our lives.

Preparation of home and heart begins to mark the season, leading to our Christmas Day celebrations. Candles burning brightly in a house suggest a warm welcome is being offered. Our homes are meant to be habitations of the heart, places of solace and welcome. Sadly, like many others, I didn't define "home" quite like that as a child.

Ours was a lonely place I longed to escape from, a site of verbal fights, resentful chill and an abiding air of animosity. I ached inside for genuine love and affection, for the right kind of attention. Maybe a soul is always seeking such things—a haven of peace and rest to feel happy in, a place where we are loved just as we are.

Whether it's a mud hut or a mansion, I believe a home is more about relationship than bricks and mortar. It should be a safe place, a shelter and sanctuary, though life can be cruel and a family not all you hoped they would be. Ideally, home should be where empty hearts, as well as empty bellies, get filled. A place of belonging, a space to be accepted, be yourself, be loved, and receive a warm welcome that never gets worn out.

As I mull over ways to make room for Jesus in this season, I marvel at God Incarnate making his home on earth, inviting us now to open our hearts and homes to him. Jesus took on frail human flesh, identified completely with our weakness, and issued an awesome invitation.

God's home, his open heart, is always open to the broken and the hurt, the lonely and the lost, the homeless and orphaned, the rootless and forgotten, those needing saving from themselves, requiring rescue and release. There is no rejection here, only unconditional love.

Heaven's only begotten Son becomes our Saviour, Brother, and Friend. We are adopted into God's family, made heirs with Christ, become children of Hope and Promise as his Holy Spirit lives within us. *How does this shape our attitude to Advent?* I believe it means actively remembering why Jesus came to earth as we search for signs of him with us in the here and now, as revealed in my poem below.

Steep descent

Watch, wait, wonder
and ponder anew
the steep descent
of Love breaking through
to our humanity,
bringing light, hope
and clarity to see
how much Father God
desires to be reunited
with you and me.

We look for the Light of his presence in a world growing darker by the day, with our hopes ignited by the thought of our Forever Home and Jesus' glorious reappearing to come. And so we read, reflect, ponder and pray, decorate, celebrate and contemplate the wonder of it all.

Most of all, we make room to receive Jesus anew. Let him be born again in our thankful hearts. We offer him a home, a place to feel welcome, a heart journeying ever closer to the spiritual homeland of his presence and a mind engaged more on the heavenly and eternal than the temporary and temporal.

Learn Religions[23] provides a helpful link you might like to check out if the practice of lighting Advent candles is new for you, as it is for me. It explains about the candles' symbolism and suggests why we might enjoy participating in this practice, especially as a family activity. And there's a lovely Advent candle liturgy[24] in the Godspace archives.

What does the word "home" conjure up for you? How might you rediscover that meaning this Advent?

Joy Lenton is a contemplative Christian writer from Norfolk, England, who suffers from M.E and multiple chronic illness. Her writing and books assist others to sense the sacred in the everyday and discover hope in painful and challenging circumstances. She would love to connect with you at her Poetry Joy and Words of Joy blogs or on Facebook.

A Mother of Sorrows - Mary's Story

by Michael Moore

When we were on our Ignatian Silent Retreat at Spring Hill College this past June, I spent a lot of time with a painting of Mary, the Mother of Jesus in the old wood-framed Sodality Chapel. This portrait was painted by Spring Hill Alumnae and Mobile, AL Artist, Stephanie Morris. The model was a Spring Hill College student. As I spent time with Mary, her eyes truly reached out and spoke to my heart and soul.

This is the final sermon in the series on The Women in Jesus's Genealogy. Three of the women were not in his Genealogy but their stories were well worth exploring. I have explored the stories and contemplated the lives of Eve (Denise preached that sermon), Ruth, Rahab, Bathsheba, The Canaanite Woman at the Well, Mary Magdalene, and now Mary, the Mother of Jesus.

As I have written and preached before, Mary is often problematic for Protestants. In part, the difficulty is in the way she is elevated in the Catholic Church. Yet many Catholic folks I know don't believe she should be elevated to the level of God any more than Protestants do. Yet as a part of the Reformation, Mary was pretty much thrown out altogether. My own journey as a Presbyterian with Mary has been challenging as well as enlightening. I have come to a deeper understanding of Mary. I truly admire her and have learned much from sitting with her. So, let's get to the subject of this final reflection in this series.

The two scripture readings that I am using tomorrow bookend the life of Jesus. In Luke 2:33-35, we hear the following somber news after Simeon blesses Jesus. In context, Jesus was brought to the Temple by his parents. Simeon was overjoyed that the long-awaited Messiah had finally come and he was alive to see it.

And the child's father and mother were amazed at what was being said about him. Then Simeon blessed them and said to Mary, "This child is destined for the falling and the rising of many in Israel, and to be a sign that will be opposed so that the inner thoughts of many will be revealed—and a sword will pierce your own soul too." (Lk 2:33-35 NRSV).

Can you imagine? As I think about Mary hearing the last part of the blessing on top of all that she had heard at Jesus's birth I am overwhelmed! "A sword will pierce your own soul too!"

As we remember the birth narrative, we can see how Mary's life with Joseph didn't exactly begin normally. They didn't have a typical betrothal. The gossip must have flown around as she began to show and as the story of God overshadowing her came out. At one point, Joseph even considered quietly divorcing her. Yet God interceded through the angelic visitors and they found their way forward as a couple.

In the birth narrative, following the visits of the Shepherds and their stories of angels, she pondered all that she had seen and heard in her heart. Forty days later the family goes to the Temple for what should be the standard purification of Mary following the birth of Jesus. Joseph and Mary were also supposed to present and dedicate their first-born son to God in order to fulfill the law in Exodus 13.

As I said earlier, when the forty-day old infant Jesus was presented to Simeon, he immediately proclaimed his joy in a very familiar passage of Scripture. Simeon took him into his arms and blessed God: "God, you can now release your servant; release me in peace as you promised. With my own eyes, I've seen your salvation; it's now out in the open for everyone to see: A God-revealing light to the non-Jewish nations, and of glory for your people Israel." (Lk 2:29-32 The Message)

There was so much for Mary to ponder in those early days. There would be so much more to ponder as Jesus grew from a baby to a young boy and finally into a man. Yet lurking in the back of her mind must have been the words of Simeon: "a sword will pierce your own soul too".

Scripture is quiet when it comes to the growing up years of Jesus. After the incident in the Temple where the twelve-year-old Jesus was amazing the religious leaders, we hear nothing about his life until he appears as a part of the crowd following John the Baptist and asks John to baptize him. The three years of Jesus's public ministry must have provided much to contemplate and be concerned about for his mother. More and more was poured into her heart as she followed Jesus, listened to his teaching, and watched the miracles.

Yet in the end, as the road led to Jerusalem for the final time, her heart must have been heavy. As the intrigue unfolded, did she remember the words of Simeon? Did she feel a pain and a piercing beginning in her heart?

The second reading from John 19:25b-30 is, I believe where her heart was pierced and broken as she watched her son dying an agonizing death on the cross. I can't even imagine the pain as Jesus looked down from the cross and said goodbye to his mother. Yet in the midst of the pain, there was a loving and tender moment as he made sure that the woman who had given birth to him and raised him would be cared for.

Meanwhile, standing near the cross of Jesus were his mother, and his mother's sister, Mary the wife of Clopas, and Mary Magdalene. When Jesus saw his mother and the disciple whom he loved standing beside her, he said to his mother, "Woman, here is your son." Then he said to the disciple, "Here is your mother." And from that hour the disciple took her into his own home (Jn 19:25b-27 NRSV).

The story has come full circle and now, with her son dying on the cross, her heart was pierced in a way it had never been pierced before. It was with this woman that I spent so much time reflecting in the Chapel at Spring Hill College. As I used the Ignatian practice of placing myself into the story, I felt her pain in a way I had never done before. During that week, I came to know Mary in a way that I hadn't in the majority of my years in ministry.

As I looked into her eyes, I saw the pain and the peace. A wise woman who was forced to learn such harsh lessons at an early age. A woman who had to watch helplessly as the Empire executed her son. A woman who had to watch as the faith community turned its back on Jesus, and in essence, on her as well. As I sat with her in the Chapel and as I have continued to do ever since, I felt a peace that I didn't expect. As I sat with her, I heard her say, "I am not God. I am the Mother of Jesus. Don't worship me. Listen to me and learn from my story."

May we do that as we consider Mary and the place she holds in the life of Jesus and in our own faith journey as well.

Michael Moore retired from the USAF where he was a Chaplain for twenty-six years. He and his wife Denise live in Carrollton, Georgia where he is the pastor of Carrollton Presbyterian Church. He blogs at https:// ScotsIrishPadre.blog and is also on the Abbey of the Arts Wisdom Council, found at: https://abbeyofthearts.com.

Waiting for a Vulnerable God

by Christine Sine

The first week of Advent has been a time of enriching reflection for me. Tom and I have taken time to go on retreat and I have spent ample time each day entering into my chosen devotionals. More than anything, I have been awed by the vulnerability of God in this Advent story, a theme that has been focused by this quote from Father Kenneth Tanner on Paul Neeley's blog:

> Christmas is not about greatness but smallness, not about strength but weakness, not about force or coercion but invitation and welcome. Christmas does not need anyone to accept its joy or embrace its light.
>
> Christmas happens in the margins, away from the spotlight. Christmas is elusive for the proud and the blustery, and threatening to every form of politics: Judean or Roman, British or Irish, Indian or Pakistani, Russian or American, Chinese or Korean, Iranian or Iraqi.
>
> Christmas is about the vulnerability of God, about the revelation that God is the servant of his universe, that if we too serve the creation with God then we join his smallness, an insignificance that displays for all to see the mystery of a profound divine weakness, a humility that casts down all greatness and arrogance and elevates poverty and lowliness.[25]

Christmas is about the vulnerability of God. What a profound observation. The One who is timeless and omnipotent becomes truly vulnerable and subject to all the created natural forces breathed into existence. The One who cannot be contained in the vast expanse of the universe is contained in the womb of a teenager, herself vulnerable – an unmarried teenager open to the censure of her society who might put her to death, risking her life as she travels to Bethlehem in the late

83

stages of her pregnancy and even more risking her life and that of her young child as she flees with Joseph into Egypt.

What incredible vulnerability. God comes not as a powerful emperor but as a babe, born not in a palace, but on the outskirts of the empire, in a small and insignificant village.

That amazingly is not the end of the story. God then invites the most vulnerable of the society into the story — the shepherds — despised and "unreliable". *Would we welcome them?*

As I ask that question, I cannot help but think of the migrant families today that are stopped at the U.S./Mexican border looking for a place where they can make a livelihood, so vulnerable and despised. Or the refugees on Lesbos in Greece, turned away by Australia and other countries. They, too, are considered unreliable, a possible threat to our security. Then I think of those who are protesting societal racial injustice. Could we welcome them as God welcomed the vulnerable?

Next come the foreigners and outsiders of another religion. They, too, could have and should have been turned away by Jesus' Jewish family. Would we have welcomed them? All of these are the vulnerable image of God – the vulnerable image that shines so brightly, not just in the Christ child, but in all those who are made in the divine image.

These are the vulnerable ones who sing for joy at the good news, who face rejection yet still come because they have caught an awe-inspiring glimpse of the One who is bigger than the universe, yet small and vulnerable in a young woman's womb.

This is our vulnerable God who gave voice and song to all creation yet became silent and inarticulate except for the cry of a baby to its mother. This is our vulnerable God who is more powerful than all the rulers of all the created worlds and yet comes as a servant to all, the One who washes feet and gives himself as a sacrifice for this creation.

This is the greatest hope that we can ever look forward to, the hope of a God who comes not in power and might but in weakness and humility. What an incredible God this God of the Universe is.

Christine describes herself as a contemplative activist, passionate gardener, author, and liturgist. She is the founder of Godspace and her most recent book is The Gift of Wonder: Creative Practices for Delighting in God.

Feeling Vulnerable

by Kate Kennington Steer

I was unable to have children of my own, so holding my nephews, niece and friends' children over the years has been such a precious bittersweet joy. As time has gone on my grief for myself has largely healed, so that now not every beautifully taut swollen pregnant belly automatically makes me want to cry or propels me from the room. I wonder if there is something about God I will never be able to understand because I am not a parent.

Yet, does that necessarily mean that 'birthing God' is reduced to being merely a metaphorical spiritual idea? Christians believe God reentered the physical universe by being born as a child. The wonder of that sentence is incalculable. The material laws of the cosmos changed when God's matter transformed into human flesh. It sounds far fetched I admit. The stuff myths are made of. But if I let the reality of this wonder incarnate in me, surely nothing will ever be impossible again. And that includes what God might want to do, in my life, with my life; how God might want to use me to draw the kingdom of heaven near — now.

However, before that possibility can take root within me, I come to a screeching mental halt: I often struggle hugely with an abiding sense that I am somehow intrinsically unloveable. Intellectually, I know this cannot be true; the love my family and friends show to me gives me practical evidence that this is not truth. Theologically, I absolutely reject the concept of original sin; the experience of holding a new born child convinces me that I too, cannot have been born with that dark baggage. The whole story of Advent reminds me time and again that God has come and is coming into the world, precisely to eliminate that lie of separation.

Sometimes, I so wish I could hold the Christ child in my arms, maybe then I would see in that child the miracle of God wanting to be brought to birth in this very specific way; maybe then I would believe I, too, am a child of God who is intimately loved and lovable; that God wants me to birth the Beloved into the world around me — now. (And

I hear Jesus whisper, "Blessed are those who do not see and yet believe").

Despite all the images that surround me at Christmas in the western northern hemisphere there is absolutely nothing sentimental about this birth of Love into Love's world. God's birthing continues to be a hard joy, a jagged light, as so many women will testify. There is always an element of danger in birthing no matter how we wrap it up in technology. So too then, I shouldn't be surprised if God's birthing in me is hard labour, long and slow in coming, requiring plenty of extensive preparation, and then demanding a long moment of absolute surrender to the process. God asks me to relinquish all my attempts at control to render myself absolutely vulnerable, just as God made the God-self vulnerable to come as a child — by choice. The risks were huge.

But sometimes I hear myself cry, "Lord, does the process have to be quite so long and so hard?"

Just as the Christ-child is made and born vulnerable in flesh, the God-child my Creator makes and bears in me is just as vulnerable in spirit. The risks are huge for this birthing too; not least that I will allow grief to harden into embittered defensiveness, or allow depression to cripple me by convincing me I am utterly alone, or allow chronic ill health to shrink my world so that I no longer seek opportunities for connecting with others or for exercising my creativity. Because even all God's power did not, and does not, make God invulnerable. God is joyful when I am joyful but equally, God is wounded when I am wounded, because that is the exactly the miracle of the incarnation which is encapsulated in the name Emmanuel: God with us.

In *The Dark Night of the Soul,* psychologist Gerald May takes this idea further, as he reflects on Teresa of Avila's contemplative vision of the Holy One needing us to love the Beloved. God's omnipotence is somehow mysteriously surrendered to, and subject, to our response to a loving God. For love always triumphs over power. And so May suggests that perhaps the true nature of what we understand as God's 'omnipotence' is not about a distant 'superpower', or even someone or something having power over us. Rather, God is precisely omnipotent because God allows the God-self to open itself to the dangers of intimacy: the intimate experience of being wounded by a lack of love, or the converse experience of being absolutely willing to be wounded for the sake of love itself, wherever and whenever love might occur. Lastly, God is willing to be wounded with those who are also willing to be wounded for the sake of loving others.[26]

God was wounded for me, God is being wounded by me. God is being wounded for me, God is being wounded with me. Out of all the murk of my muddy soul, this feels like the beginnings of a revelation. I may not be a parent but perhaps my experiences of being made vulnerable physically, mentally and spiritually by chronic ill health brings its particular understandings of God's character with it too. Perhaps me becoming a host-space for God, a Light-bearer, is perhaps not out of the question either.

Perhaps by embracing my vulnerability is how, finally, I learn to live loved.

Kate Kennington Steer is a writer, photographer and visual artist, with a deep abiding passion for how spirituality might be revealed, received and expressed through creativity in general and contemplative photography in particular. Every now and then she wonders about these things at her shot at ten paces and image into ikon blogs and her Facebook project Acts of Daily Seeing.

St. Lucy's Day – December 13

by Carol Dixon

My Swedish pen-friend and I began corresponding when we were twelve years old and we continue to keep in touch sixty years on (these days usually by email) and it was interesting and exciting to learn about each other's customs and traditions especially at special times of the year. It was from her I first heard about the lovely tradition of Luciadagen – Saint Lucy's Day, when the light of Christ conquering the darkness is celebrated. This is what she told me about the festival.

Tradition has it that Lucia is to wear 'light in her hair', which in practice means a crown of electric candles in a wreath on her head. Lucia wears a white gown with a red ribbon around her waist. Each of her handmaidens carries a candle too. The star boys, who, like the handmaidens, are dressed in white gowns, carry stars on sticks and have tall paper cones on their heads. The gingerbread men bring up the rear, carrying small lanterns. There is always a special atmosphere in the morning of Lucia day when the lights are dimmed and the sound of the singing grows as the Lucia procession enters the room. Schools and old people's homes and other institutions have a Lucia procession. All Swedes know the Lucia song by heart and many Lucia songs have the same theme:

'The night treads heavily around yards and dwellings
In places unreached by the sun, the shadows brood.
Into our dark house she comes, bearing lighted candles, Saint Lucia, Saint Lucia.'

St Lucia lived around 280 AD and came from Sicily. She was known for her charity to the Christians hiding in the catacombs to avoid persecution. Lucy wore candles in her hair to leave her hands free to carry food to those in need. Missionaries to the Vikings brought her story to the far north and her feast day is celebrated in both the Roman Catholic and Lutheran churches.

St Lucia's day was originally celebrated on the winter solstice, the darkest day of the year as a reminder that even in the deepest darkness the light of Christ shines.

I discovered, too, that when the elderly people in the village who live alone receive a visit from St Lucia and her attendants, they are often given a special surprise: a small gift of food — ginger biscuits and sweet saffron flavoured buns 'Lucia katter' in the shape of curled up cats with raisin eyes and are invited to join in the singing.

This reminded me of the lovely old hymn "Surprised by Joy" by William Cowper.

> Sometimes a light surprises
> the Christian while s/he sings;
> it is the Lord who rises
> with healing in his wings:
> when comforts are declining,
> he grants the soul again
> a season of clear shining,
> to cheer it after rain.

The 18th century poet and hymn writer, William Cowper suffered from mental illness and went through many periods of spiritual darkness yet his writing speaks of God's love shining through. A poem of his (which became the hymn "God moves in a mysterious way his wonders to perform") was written after a suicide attempt and is entitled "Light shining out of darkness".

In Advent, we read many encouraging passages from the Bible concerning the coming of light and hope. Isaiah surprised his fellow exiles in Babylon with his words of God's promise: "The people who walked in darkness have seen a great light" (Isa. 9:2) and John in his Gospel (Jn 1:4-9), tells of the fruition of the promise in the coming of Jesus, a reading we often hear in church at this time of year.

Jesus himself told the people of his time who walked in the darkest of foreign oppression "I have come into the world so that no one who believes in me should stay in darkness." (Jn 12:46) and St Paul in times of persecution wrote to the Corinthian Christians (in 2 Cor. 4:6), "For God who said, 'let light shine out of darkness' made his light shine in our hearts to give us the light of the knowledge of God's glory displayed in the face of Christ'."

Advent gives us a wonderful opportunity to share the light of Christ with those around us, to surprise our friends and neighbours with the message of the light of Christ in dark times as one of my favourite children's' hymn reminds us.

Jesus bids us shine with a pure, clear light,
like a little candle burning in the night.
In the world is darkness, so we must shine,
you in your small corner, and I in mine.
Jesus bids us shine, first of all for him;
well he sees and knows it if our light grows dim.
He looks down from heaven to see us shine,
you in your small corner, and I in mine.
Jesus bids us shine, then, for all around;
many kinds of darkness in this world are found:
sin and want and sorrow; so we must shine,
you in your small corner, and I in mine.[27]

A couple of years ago, I wrote an Advent prayer after hearing Bernadette Farrell's beautiful song, "Christ be our light".

Festival of Light – Advent
Come, loving God,
into our worship and into our world;
Come with the light of love,
Come with the light of peace,
Come with the light of hope.
Come, loving God,
into our worship and into our world
and banish the darkness of night
with the dawn of your coming.

Carol Dixon from the UK is a United Reformed Church lay preacher and writes hymns for the Iona Community Wild Goose Publications, HymnQuest, and Church of Scotland Hymnary 4. She enjoys spending time with her grandchildren & touring with her husband in their caravette.

Advent Vulnerability

by Keren Dibbens-Wyatt

When I contemplate becoming like the Christ child, vulnerability is the first thing that comes to mind and heart.

That God's child might begin again as all his children do, as a baby growing within a womb, is almost too astonishing to take in. Truly it is a thing of wonder, that the one through whom the Universe was created would become incarnate in such a vulnerable fashion.

To begin with, getting from conception (even by the Holy Spirit) to birth is a long and perilous journey. So many tiny lives that don't make it, for whatever reason. God signed himself up to that, he came into even that possibility. He opened himself up to that kind of pain, to death itself. In a way, that was what was always going to happen, because the world would kill Jesus one way or another. And you might say, that's ridiculous, God knew he would be born, it was foretold. Maybe. But it was risky all the same. He chose that.

What if Mary's parents had forced her to eat certain herbs because they were afraid of shame? What if they had disowned her? What if Joseph had not listened to the angel and left her all alone in the world? What if she had said no to God's request?

The "what ifs" are endless, which is partly why pregnant women feel vulnerable too. Their bodies are doing something new and amazing, they are pouring all their strength into a love that is yet unknown, for a person who will change their lives forever. In a way, that is how we all begin to experience Christ growing within us. As Eckhart famously said, "We are all meant to be mothers of God, for God is always needing to be born." The world needs the Incarnation now as ever, Christ's body to be unified and loving, nurturing and tending the world he helped create.

Jesus stayed with those who were vulnerable his whole life and ministry. He opened his heart up to those who were weary of the system, who didn't have any power, who were the lowest in status. I've seen a few articles recently telling us that this vulnerability which is being talked about now, largely due to the research and popularity of sociologist Brené Brown, is not about weakness. That it requires strength to be truly vulnerable, to lay ourselves open to the risk of a powerful honesty that might get us hurt. That's true. But it *is* also about weakness. It is about siding with the small, living and suffering with us in our uncertainty and inability.

The vulnerability of the manger, like the vulnerability of the cross, is pure love. A love that says, I will go through this with you. That says, I could opt out of your suffering, but I choose to share it. I lay down my birth, my life, my death, for you.

I refuse to speak because no one gave you a voice. I refuse to fight back because you could not. I refuse to use the power of angels for my salvation, because you, too, were helpless.

God with us, Immanuel.

"But he said to me, 'My grace is sufficient for you, for my power is made perfect in weakness.' Therefore I will boast all the more gladly about my weaknesses, so that Christ's power may rest on me" (2 Cor. 12:9).

Keren Dibbens-Wyatt is a chronically ill writer and artist with a passion for poetry, mysticism, story and colour. Her writing features regularly on spiritual blogs and in literary journals. She is the author of the book Recital of Love (Paraclete Press 2020), lives in South East England and is mainly housebound by her illness.

Good News of Great Joy

by Kate Kennington Steer

> *Although the wind*
> *blows terribly here,*
> *the moonlight also leaks*
> *between the roof planks*
> *of this ruined house.*
>
> Izumi Shikibu (974?-1034?) [tr. Jane Hirshfield / Mariko Aratani]

Jesus sat down to chat, to eat, to sleep in a wide variety of houses. He invited the strangest mix of society to join him. I can imagine the dismay of many of his hosts at the steady influx and invasion of unknown people, not dressed for the occasion, smelling rather ripe and rank, with dirt on their clothes and mud on their sandals. A mix of people who were associated with radical religious movements, social extremists, and political agitators might well cause severe anxiety to a host who feared for their reputation and association.

But this is what Jesus calls hospitality - hospitality to others and hospitality to ourselves. No one is to be shut out.

At present, I cannot offer anyone a meal or a home, since illness often prevents me socialising in the way I would like, and I have no home at the moment to invite others into. What I can do from my bed is work on my own prejudices, those attitudes that would stop me in the future from even seeing the presence of someone who might be in need of the kind of hospitality I could offer. On his blog[28], Pete Grieg, the leader of the 24/7 Prayer movement and the Emmaus Church in Guidlford, England, reminds me that spiritual hospitality is not the same as giving dinner parties, which, he quips, is not the gift of hospitality but the gift of a box of chocolates. By contrast, biblical hospitality is heartfelt and requires sacrificial thoughtfulness, flexibility, patience and consistency. The gift of hospitality calls us to be imaginative in our response: because above all, the gift of spiritual hospitality, requires us to listen. Such listening, according to Henri Nouwen, aims not to change people, but to offer others whatever space they might need for change to take place.

Listening to those who come sit at the end of my bed is something I can do. The vision that my 'sick room' could become a temple of transfigurative encounter gives me real hope.

But will I be ready when the world comes to me? Am I prepared to hear the hard stuff, or am I so ground down by the fogged vision of depression and illness that I am unwilling to hear anyone else's sadness or joy?

I am still learning that in order to provide exquisite hospitality to those who come to me, I need to bestow the same precious gift on my inner political agitator Kate, the one who gets cross and shouty; on the really awkward, angular Kate who hasn't grown up from a gawky introspective teenager yet; on the flamboyant, arrogant Kate who flaunts her superior learning in everyone's face; on the seductress Kate, who enacts dark shadowy fantasies that entrap and deplete all vital energies… These are the Kates I really don't want to admit even exist within me, let alone spend any time with them listening to them. But that is what Jesus asks me to do at the start of another year on the Way of Wisdom.

And I will not be alone. For the advent of Jesus into the world is all about this one central fact: God is with me. God is with us.

So there is no need to slam the door and shun who I fear will be harmful company within myself.

I recently reread Psalm 31:22 (NRSV) and heard the psalmist's panic attack echo in my own fears that arise from believing the lie of isolation: "I had said in my alarm, '" am driven far from your sight.' But you heard my supplications when I cried out to you for help."

In the midst of depression, it feels like I am completely alone, cut off from God, from others, even from myself. But part of extending Jesus's model of hospitality even to myself, is to remember that this is the opposite of true reality. All I need do is listen to those who cry out in me, and join in with their cry to God for help.

Can I open enough doors in myself today so that the cries of the wounded in the world join the cries of the wounded within myself? Can we who weep come together to God to receive the wholeness of being heard?

This is the Good News of Great Joy that we await expectantly together through this longest night.

Kate Kennington Steer is a writer, photographer and visual artist, with a deep abiding passion for how spirituality might be revealed, received and expressed through creativity in general and contemplative photography in particular. Every now and then she wonders about these things at her shot at ten paces and image into ikon blogs and her Facebook project Acts of Daily Seeing.

Week 3 of Advent: Living

In Hope

I Choose to Look at the World with Joy

by Christine Sine

I choose to look at the world with joy,
to enjoy the glory of the
everlasting, ever present One.
I choose to embrace what
delights God's heart,
and breath in the fragrance of God's love.
I choose to listen to the whispers of God's voice,
calling me to slow down and take notice.
I choose to look at the world with joy,
and absorb the wonder of divine presence.
I choose to delight in the Creator of all things
and relish the delight God takes in me.

Hope Overflowing

by Sue Duby

When friends ask me if I'm a morning or night person, I'm used to letting out a sigh with a wink and smile…"Actually, neither one! I just like to sleep!". It must be in the gene pool. Krista and Peter both blessed me as a young Mama with 3-hour naps. I'm grateful for the gift of sleeping deep and hard most nights, though waking can be a determined choice!

These days, as I move through relaxed morning pre-coffee fog, it hits me. . . again. . . just like the movie Groundhog Day. . . and my senses sharpen realizing it's still here. This crazy season of isolation, masks, opening up, mixed directives and missing hanging out with friends and family. Each day, I'm expectantly waiting for a gentle reminder that He's present, in the midst and not surprised.

This morning heading for the kitchen, my eye fixed on a Mother's Day gift from years ago. A painted frame of text, with colors that just happened to match my favorite chair. I knew I had my focus for the day.

"May the God of hope fill you with all joy and peace as you trust in Him…" (Rom. 15:13).

Wow… just a bit of pondering and I could sense the challenge to embrace a shift in focus. From news, statistics and predictions that induce worry, to simple truth that produces a lighter step and smile. Back to some basics that lead to light-hearted wake-up mornings!

- God IS the God of hope. The very author and anchor of hope. The one who makes it possible for us to have "favorable and confident expectation; happy anticipation of the good"[29] even with an unseen future.

- God desires to FILL us. So somehow, though I need to listen, follow and obey, He is the one to gift that hope, joy and peace to me. I can't muster it up on my own. I picture an empty jar (me) and God holding a pitcher of hope, ready to pour it and fill me.

- The nature of His hope (not my own created version) releases joy and peace in that filling. His hope is certain, powerful and alive.

- In the midst, I do have one task to do. All of the above happens "as you trust in Him". An ongoing, journeying kind of task… "as you trust". . . along the way, in each moment, with each step. Believing He is able. Knowing His desire is to "load-lift" and bring me gladness of heart, because He loves me. Choosing trust as my stance before Him, with Him.

Paul goes further to remind us that God's not only in the business of taking care of my heart. Rather, this amazing God of Hope fills us, "so that you may overflow with hope by the power of the Holy Spirit". Purpose in the gift, not just for myself, but for all those around me.

Picture that same pitcher filled to the brim and spilling over. The slightest bump and more comes forth. For those He brings near. In conversation. In prayer for others. As I write a note to a friend or send a text to my kids. A sprinkling, even soaking of hope, joy and peace (all His). In my trusting and believing who He is… that amazing God of Hope. He does the filling, that allows the spilling over.

What a refreshing delight to think that our lives can be "hope, joy and peace spillers" in the midst of crazy uncertainty! Lord, show us how to daily receive a fresh filling from You, the God of Hope, so that all that You are might spill over from our lives to others. With gladness of heart and gratefulness for who You are. To encourage others in their journeys, as You have in mine.

Sue grew up on an island minutes from downtown Seattle. After adventures teaching high school math and thirty years with faith-based non-profits (Mercy Ships and Hope Force International), she retired in NW Arkansas with husband Chuck. She loves travel (thirty-threecountries and counting), flower arranging, sweet friendship with children, Krista & Peter & their spouses, grandson hugs, creating and coffee shops.

Wrapped in God's Love

by Lilly Lewin

The few weeks before Christmas are filled with to-do lists and expectations. For some, it means traveling to visit friends and family. For others, it means working longer hours at restaurants, stores, and churches. Some to-do lists are fun, and involve things like making cookies and wrapping gifts, while others bring more stress and anxiety, more frustration and less rest.

In the midst of these busy days, I invite you take time to rest in God's love for you.

Use the image of Mary holding Jesus and wrapping him in swaddling clothes to help you connect with God's love holding you, and protecting you. Use a painting (find one online) that resonates with you, to help you with this. Ponder this image. What do you see? What do you notice? How does Mary look at Jesus? How does Jesus want to look at you? Use these images to pray with this week.

Imagine Mary, holding Jesus in her arms and singing him a lullaby. *What if Jesus wants to sing a song of love and comfort to you in these days of Advent and into Christmas? Can you hear him? What Song is Jesus singing to you?* Find a lullaby and play it as a reminder of God's love holding you close.

Imagine how safe a baby feels in their mother's arms. Allow yourself to be held in the arms of God. *How does it feel to be held and comforted? Will you allow Jesus to hold you in the days ahead?*

Put a blanket around your shoulders. Let the blanket remind you of Mary wrapping her baby in swaddling clothes to keep him warm and protected. Sit with this image. As Mary wrapped Jesus in swaddling clothes, allow Jesus to wrap you in his love this holiday season. **Each time you wrap up in a blanket to watch TV, read a book, or add a blanket to your bed for warmth, allow this to be a symbol of Jesus wrapping you his blanket of love and safety.**

The blanket is symbol of the love of Jesus surrounding you. The blanket is a symbol of Jesus holding you close and loving you just as you are!

Be wrapped in God's love this Christmas. As Mary wrapped Jesus in bands of cloth, let the love of Jesus wrap around you and remove the stress and fear, the anxiety and expectations others.

Allow God to hold you close, like a mother holds her child.

Breathe in Love
Breathe out fear.
Breathe in Belovedness.
Breathe out self doubt.

Breathe in love for the unique creation you are.Breathe out comparison.

Breathe in Love.
Breathe out stress.

Breathe in Love.
Rest in this great Love.
Be wrapped in it!
Merry Christmas!

Lilly is a worship curator, speaker, author, artist, and founder of thinplaceNASHVILLE, and freerangeworship.com She creates sacred space prayer experiences and leads workshops & retreats across the country and beyond. She writes the freerangefriday blog each week at Godspacelight.com

Come Thou Unexpected Jesus

by Christine Sine

When Advent begins, Tom and I have pulled out our Advent music. One of my favourite Advent hymns is *Come Thou Long Expected Jesus* with music by Rowland H. Prichard and lyrics by Charles Wesley. However, this year I find myself singing *come thou unexpected Jesus*. The Jews were waiting for a Messiah but not one like this. Nothing about the birth of Jesus was what they expected. At the centre is Mary, who conceives as an unwed teenager, Joseph, who accepts a child not his own and Elizabeth, who welcomes and supports her cousin through what must have been a harrowing first few months of her pregnancy. All of them living at the outskirts of the empire, unknown by the priests and rulers in Jerusalem, unimportant in the political and religious scene of the day.

So many good reasons for Mary to be afraid when the angel Gabriel comes to visit. Her world, in fact, the whole world, was about to be changed and she was centre stage.

Gabriel appeared to her and said, "Greetings! You are favored, and the Lord is with you! Among all women on the earth, you have been blessed." Mary was deeply troubled over the words of the angel and bewildered over what this may mean for her.[30] But the angel reassured her, saying, "Mary, don't be afraid. You have found favor with God." (Lk 1:28-30 The Voice).

Advent disrupted everything in the life of Mary, Joseph and Elizabeth. It should disrupt everything in our lives, too, as we look in hope and anticipation towards the coming of the One through whom God and the entire creation will once more be fully united.

So often we hope for change in our lives and our world, wanting to see that better world of God's promises come into being, but when God suggests that we could be the instruments of that change, we draw back afraid to step out of our comfort zones. We want change to happen without us needing to do anything. After all, we are small and insignificant players in God's plan. How could we possibly be the instruments of change that God is looking for?

As I wait with Mary for the birth of Jesus this Advent season, I look around at a world that desperately needs change. We face a climate crisis that will devastate our world if we don't make radical changes to our lifestyles. We face the pall of COVID-19, political upheaval and economic turmoil in ways that I have not seen before in my lifetime. It is easy for fear and anxiety to rear their ugly heads and hold us captive.

God comes to all of us in so many unexpected ways, asking us to be the change the world needs to see. I think that Mary, in some ways, represents all of us — unsettled by what God's messengers have said, yet needing to embrace our call to be instruments of change without yielding to our fears. We do indeed need to make room for Christ to be born afresh in our hearts and in our lives this year in ways that can help change our world.

So what do we do during this season of waiting?

- **Listen to the angels.** We may not have heavenly visitors come to us, but there are other messengers that God sends to help us find our way to the Messiah – environmentalists like Greta Thunberg, racial activists like Dr. Brenda Salter McNeil and contemplatives like Richard Rohr who know that there needs to be change in the world and call us to be the instruments of that change. Who are the angels, who are messengers of change and new birth for you?

- **Look for the Elizabeths.** When God calls, who do we run to? All of us need supporters like Joseph and Elizabeth who can help keep God's dreams alive during the seasons of hard waiting that we face. Who are the ones that support you and encourage you when God's call comes and you are afraid?

- **Don't be afraid of the unexpected.** Like Mary we need to be willing to be instruments of change without yielding to our fears and anxieties. God finds delight in all of us and promises us a special gift — not necessarily a baby born in a manger but a fresh touch of the divine presence born in our hearts and in our minds. Are we willing to let go of our expectations for this season and allow God to reveal something new to us?

What Is Your Response?

Sit quietly and prayerfully with your eyes closed and listen to the song *Come Thou Long Expected Jesus*[30]. Instead of long expected Jesus, read unexpected Jesus. What comes to your mind? Is there something unexpected that God is wanting to give birth to in you this year? What is one action step you could take as Christmas approaches to make this possible?

Christine describes herself as a contemplative activist, passionate gardener, author, and liturgist. She is the founder of Godspace and her most recent book is The Gift of Wonder: Creative Practices for Delighting in God.

Hope

by Hilary Horn

As Christmas approaches and our advent season has arrived, one word that has been sticking out to me in particular is the word **hope**.

What I think is so different from the hope that the world presents us, is that hope in the bible is not just happy optimism but a choice to wait on God to bring about a future. This feeling of tension and expectation as we wait because we know God's past faithfulness is what motivates us to look forward in the hope we have in Him. We trust nothing other than God's character.

As a mother, I can only imagine Mary during this time. Many young woman have a hope (this happy optimism) in our future. For many of us, that involves hope for a future spouse and most likely children. We daydream about what our life may look like, what we hope it does many years down the road. Two kids? Maybe three? Six? Maybe we hope to own a house, have some sort of stability in our careers. Maybe we want a natural birth. We scroll Pinterest and get way over our heads on all the baby stuff we want to get one day and how we want to decorate our nursery. We think of things like clothe diapers or disposable? Breastfed or bottles? We dream of what our child could be, what they may look like. Will they have my eyes or their dad's? Will they be funny or sensible? You wonder endlessly.

Then, often our perfect optimistic dreams are jaded. Life happens and most of us don't always get the ideals we dreamt of.

Mary sure didn't.

She was a young, single mother at first. No husband. No home. No stability. She was probably afraid, ostracized and abandoned. She went off to her cousins house. I'm sure she was worried more about the outcome of her life, let alone what crib she wanted to purchase. She didn't even have a clue what to dream up about the incarnate God and what he would look like. Would this baby even look or be like her?

But one thing she did have. She had the living hope of Jesus in her. A hope that isn't just a feeling of optimism, a hope that can be crushed.

But a hope that is an eternal, a faithful hope. A hope of who God is and what he will do.

She lived and breathed the waiting tension and expectation of hope. She knew she carried the savior of the world. What a weight! To mother Jesus? Can you imagine this young girl's thoughts? But she trusted full-heartedly in who God was in the past and who she knew he was going to be in the future.

She resinates the hope in her soul when she proclaims this song in Luke 1:46-55:

> My soul glorifies the Lord
> [47] and my spirit rejoices in God my Savior,
> [48] for he has been mindful
> of the humble state of his servant.
> From now on all generations will call me blessed,
> [49] for the Mighty One has done great things for me—
> holy is his name.
> [50] His mercy extends to those who fear him,
> from generation to generation.
> [51] He has performed mighty deeds with his arm;
> he has scattered those who are proud in their inmost thoughts.
> [52] He has brought down rulers from their thrones
> but has lifted up the humble.
> [53] He has filled the hungry with good things
> but has sent the rich away empty.
> [54] He has helped his servant Israel,
> remembering to be merciful
> [55] to Abraham and his descendants forever,
> just as he promised our ancestors.

She remembered God's faithfulness, his mercy and power. And she was confident in the hope for what was her future and the baby that she now carried. Even though her life was in what most of us would see as utter shambles — she trusted in the hope because she knew Gods past faithfulness and his future. She even called herself blessed.

Whatever season you are in — a joyful one or maybe one that looks like unmet expectations, chaotic, broken, afraid, and alone...

We may not have the hope that the world gives us, but we can be confident in the hope that God is.

Jesus is our living, eternal hope. I am choosing to hope and wait in this tension for the now and not yet Kingdom until he returns once again.

So as advent continues, I am reminded that hope is not that God guarantees a life of bliss and perfection, but that in all seasons, trials and circumstances, God is with us.

In seasons that are hard, I want to proclaim the truth of God's promises and be like Mary, calling myself, "blessed" because I rest in the biblical hope of Jesus… God with us.

Hilary Horn is an international justice advocate and lover of all things creative. She is on the staff team at Mill Creek Foursquare church, on top of hustling two little boys.

Seeds in the Sidewalk

by James Amadon

The news hangs from my shoulders these days like a heavy backpack, each story another stone to carry. I am tired of paying attention but afraid to stop, and it is taking a toll. My wife, Emily, says she can tell I am carrying the weight of the world when my shoulders start to slump forward. It is hard to stand up straight when each day brings new revelations of the terrible things that happen when selfishness and fear is wedded to power. Even now, as I write this in my local coffee shop, a young, white man with a shaved head is loudly pontificating to his companion about genetics and Martin Luther King, Jr. I cannot tell for sure if he is part of the increasingly vocal ethno-nationalist movement in our nation, but it is a sad sign that this is my first guess.

One of the significant victims of our current cultural moment is joy, the deep sense that, come what may, the heart of the world contains an unshakeable goodness that calls forth gratitude and hope. This is what we hear in the opening poetry of Genesis, when God declares again and again and again, "It is good" (Gen. 1). Joy is rooted in memory and sustained by hope; neither comes as naturally to me as I would like. I take it as a great grace that, despite my inclination to forget the past and fear for the future, joy wedges into the present like seeds in a cracked sidewalk, unexpectedly shooting up blessings in a concrete world. This was true the other day as I watched the literal sidewalk in my neighborhood shimmer in post-rain sunshine underneath a vibrant sky awash in grays and blues. It was a moment that transcended the moment, and it filled me with enough joy to lift my shoulders, shed my burdens, and open my eyes to something deeper.

Joy also came unexpectedly three years ago when I was given the opportunity to become the Executive Director of Mustard Seed Associates, the not-for-profit from which Godspace was birthed. I have been filled with hope as I help shape Circlewood[31], the name we have given to the new ministry focus of MSA. We are working with Christ-followers and like-minded friends to accelerate the transition of humanity into life-giving inhabitants of creation. This mission stems from the heavy realization of how much damage we have done to God's world and the uncertain future that lies before us. But it is focused on what we can do in the present moment — how we can become seeds of hope in our cracked culture, rooted in the hope that all of creation is being woven into God's redemptive love and grace.

It is this hope that keeps me from allowing the bad news of the day to overshadow the good news of Jesus. This good news burst into the world two millennia ago, dazzling lowly shepherds in the Palestinian countryside with a message that reaches through time to speak the truth we need to hear this Advent: "Do not be afraid. I bring you good news that will cause great joy for all the people" (Lk 2:10).

Great joy such as this is often accompanied by great sorrow, and those who follow Jesus know that the child in the manger becomes the outlaw on the cross, shoulders slumped in death from carrying the weight of the world. But Jesus, "who for the sake of the joy that was set before him endured the Cross" (Heb. 12:2), was buried like a seed in the cracked earth and burst forth as the first sign of God's new creation.

It may be tempting this Advent to see only leafless trees, falling sunlight, and a darkening cultural horizon full of division, destruction, and death. But this is God's pattern: death to life, bad news to good, sorrow to joy. Lift up your shoulders, shed your burdens, plant your seeds, and open your eyes to the joy that springs up in unlikely places.

James Amadon is new executive director of Circlewood, and the Executive Producer of the Earthkeepers Podcast. In addition to his leadership skills and experience, he brings a passion for helping people see the personal, social, and ecological dimensions of faith and developing ways to integrate these dimensions into an integrated whole. Learn more about Circlewood at www.circlewood.online, and feel free to reach out to James at james.amadon@circlewood.online.

Ready or Not, Here I Come

by Jenneth Graser

Read Isaiah 42:14, John 3:6, Romans 8:24-25

At certain times in our life, we become aware of the fact that God is preparing to release us into a new season. It feels as though we have come to the moment of birth. God placed a seed of this season in us a while ago; it has been growing for quite some time and now we feel he is about to bring it forth. We can imagine how Mary must have felt, keeping what she was told inside her heart, believing what was promised. The experience she had of meeting Elizabeth when they were both pregnant, released a burst of prophetic praise out of her that revealed the great anticipation she must have felt housing the King of kings in her womb. The preparation for these new seasons is like incubating the life of Jesus in us for a whole new expression and time of his coming in our lives. We become the place of growth as we wait in anticipation for all the good things he has prepared in advance for us. "That is why waiting does not diminish us, any more than waiting diminishes a pregnant mother. We are enlarged in the waiting. We, of course, don't see what is enlarging us. But the longer we wait, the larger we become, and the more joyful our expectancy." (Romans 8:24-25 The Message).

It is during these times that we hold onto the life-giving words of Jesus. As we meditate on his promises and inheritance, we become enlarged in the waiting and become more and more ready for the time of "birth". And when we find ourselves launched out into new things, we continue to rely completely on him and contemplate the wonders of what he has done in our hearts. "Mary treasured up all these things and pondered them in her heart" (Lk 2:19).

Thank you Lord, that I am enlarged through the times of waiting for your purposes to be born through me. I will treasure the dreams and visions you give as a sign of what is to come and ponder them with you. I know when the time comes for this season to be born, that nothing can hold it back!

111

Ready or not, here I come

On the updraft of a dream
Joel paints the picture for you
Visions, all for men and women
Young and old, and it's coming.

I crescendo off the embankment
Of birth readiness
A waterslide rush headlong
Into new things, new times
New seasons, everything new.

I am the woman of birth readiness
I hold the dreams of my internal child.
Surely "Christ in me" takes on a whole
New meaning; ready or not
Here I come.

I imagine the Christ child living in me
Christ the Man, the Resurrected King
All as much part of me
As I am of him.

I hold up my hands like wings,
Heaven's basin is my resting place.
All of my prayers resonate with the sound
Of voices, forming incense, now rising
To the ears, voice, nose of the one who loves me so[32]

*Jenneth and Karl, together with their three daughters, live in a seaside village
of the Western Cape, South Africa. She shares a spirit of healing and hope
through her writings and contemplative music
at www.secretplacedevotion.weebly.com*

How It Ends

by Ana Lisa de Jong

We are stories within a story.
Narratives within the larger Word.
Even while we question meaning or reason,
we have comfort in knowing how it ends.
More than players on a stage,
we have our own self-determination.
We are safe to make decisions and choices,
within the provision of an all-encompassing plan.
Advent reminds us of the eternal story,
in which life and death take turns
in entering from the wings.
And nothing in this world is ever final
while the Word has the enduring say.
We are stories within a story.
Narratives within the larger Word.
Even while we wonder at the purpose of our griefs,
with relief we keep our trust in joy's return.
For Advent teaches us the story within the story.
The larger volume and the smallest detail contained.
Held together in a great unfolding scroll
by hands that reach from beginning to end.
Advent recalls to us the gift of waiting.
The treasure held close to Mary's breast.
The heart already leaps for what isn't yet,
this comfort is knowing how it ends.
The hope in which we, waiting,
place our faith.
The trust in what we know
has been conceived.

Ana Lisa de Jong is a poet from Aotearoa, New Zealand, 'Land of the Long White Cloud'. She is the author of five published poetry collections, and generously gives away smaller collections to readers online. Read more: www.livingtreepoetry.com.

Week 4 of Advent: Lean Towards the Light

When God Gave Us Jesus

by Mary Harwell Sayler

– the One Who would save us –
Heaven could not contain itself.

Light spilled from a star,
heralding His arrival.

The earth burst into life.
Birds called for revival.

Morning Glories began
to bloom in the night chill,

and frightened
shepherds
trembled like sheep
while angels
awakened sleep
with songs
as light as snowflakes,
as powerful as a
Tsunami of harmony
pouring onto the earth
at Jesus' birth.

Oh, praise Him![33]

Poet, writer, and lifelong student of the Bible, Mary Harwell Sayler writes in all genres for Christian, educational, and indie publishers. Recently she collected actual prayers from God's word into the Book of Bible Prayers then researched God's promises for the book, Kneeling on the Promises of God. Her poetry book, A Gathering of Poems, collects many of her poems from previously published works.

Light Emerges Out of Darkness

by Christine Sine

> In the beginning the Word already existed.
> The Word was with God,
> and the Word was God.
> 2 He existed in the beginning with God.
> 3 God created everything through him,
> and nothing was created except through him.
> 4 The Word gave life to everything that was created
> and his life brought light to everyone.
> 5 The light shines in the darkness,
> and the darkness can never extinguish it. (Jn 1:1-5 NLT)

I read these words as Tom and I took off from Seattle for an early morning flight to Pennsylvania several years ago. Then I looked outside the window and was awed by the sunrise over Mt Rainier – light emerging in the darkness. As we flew back to Seattle a couple of days later, we landed as the sun was setting. I looked out the window to see a brilliant golden sunset greeting me. Wow — not only does the light shine in the darkness of the dawn but it also illumines the darkness of the sunset. So much hope and promise in these images. Such powerful reminders, bringers of hope and anticipation to my soul. Light DOES shine in the darkness, I thought and NOTHING will extinguish it.

As we head towards Christmas through the last days of Advent it is so reassuring to know that nothing will ever extinguish the light of God, neither in our hearts and in our world.

This year seems to have been filled with so much darkness — so many deaths from COVID that we have lost count; so much shock at the horrors of racial injustice, so much heartache for migrant families hoping for a new life in countries that do not want them; hurricanes, droughts, fires that have extinguished life before its time, the threats of climate change, political upheaval and animosity have all overwhelmed us, often with despair. The darkness seems to shroud our world and drain our hope.

No wonder I really crave light more than ever this year. No wonder my morning practice of lighting the candles in my circle of light each day brings both joy and comfort. They connect me in a special way to my family, friends and neighbours near and far as well as to special places and God's beautiful light-filled created world.

As I sit in my circle of light, I am reminded that white light is not really white at all, it is made up of all the colours of the rainbow. It reminds me that in Jesus, too, are all the colours of the rainbow. And that has me searching, not just for physical light but for the light of Christ in beautiful images from different cultures - Ethiopian icons, and black madonnas, He Qi's Chinese images and Hanna Varghese's Malaysian images, Jesus Mafa scenes from the Cameroons. I particularly love to browse Paul Neeley's site Global Christian Worship[34] for Christmas music and images from around the world at this time of year. This has connected me in an even deeper way to the Christ light and the richness of God's children "from every tribe and nation".

Now I sit and meditate on John O'Donohue's words in his book, *Beauty: The Invisible Embrace,*

> The very breath of life breathes into things until their individual colours flame. Such is the generosity of air, self-effacing and unseen it asks nothing of the eye, yet it offers life to the invisible fields where light can unfold its scriptures of colour. We dwell between the air and the earth, guests of that middle kingdom where light and colour embrace.[35]

As I ponder different cultural images of Christ's birth, I sit in awe of the rainbow hues that make up the light of Christ. I do feel I live in that place between the air and the earth, guests of that middle kingdom where light and colour embrace. I realize I will never appreciate the light of Christ until I fully embrace the colours of God's rainbow of joy that are all the tribes and nations and cultures of our earth.

What Is Your Response?

Visit Paul Neeley's website and browse his collection of Asian and African Christian art[36]. What impresses you about the Jesus you see depicted in these images? What do these images teach you about the coming of Christ into our world?

Yet there is hope. God's newness is emerging and will one day burst into our world like the sun rising in a new dawn. That is the hope of Advent and the promise of Christmas that still shines brightly in our hearts and in the dark dawn of our lives.

Christine describes herself as a contemplative activist, passionate gardener, author, and liturgist. She is the founder of Godspace and her most recent book is The Gift of Wonder: Creative Practices for Delighting in God.

Becoming a Beacon

by Keren Dibbens-Wyatt

As regular readers at Godspace know, I am severely affected by M.E. Sometimes I feel as though my chronic illness is like a wicked witch in a fairy tale, keeping me captive in a tall tower. I remain attached to this analogy despite the fact that I live in a bungalow, and am definitely a very long way from being a princess. My hair has grown very long over the last few years of being unwell enough to get it cut or styled, but I don't particularly relish the idea of anyone climbing up it. I get more than my share of neck pain as it is. But yes, all joking aside, I do feel shut away from the world, held in a world of living mostly in one room against my will, and almost completely dependent on my uncomplaining, constant husband. And though I am particularly bad this year, I've been cloistered to varying degrees for over twenty years.

It is hard, often, to imagine what God is playing at in all this. Why doesn't he just heal me? I would love to go for long walks. That is the thing I grieve for most, my walking. At best now, I stumble a few times a day from the bedroom to the living room, from the bedroom to the bathroom. The outside world is a closed one to me, bar the occasional daring jaunt to the patio.

I have had to ask myself some difficult questions about the worth of my life. I pray a lot, and I ask God about this too. What is the point of such a life? Is there light shining here too, in this darkness?

I have taken Julian of Norwich as a kind of mentor, someone who chose to be shut away, anchored to one place, in order to free up her time for God, and the work of meditating on all the wonderful visions he had given her. I have received a lot from the Lord too, albeit minuscule in comparison, for we are all given the tasks we are capable of. I've been given seeings and stories, poems and prayers, and creative talents I never knew were in me.

This time, albeit robbed of the blessings that I hoped would be mine at this stage of life, and despite my often feeling low, is nevertheless full of light. Ideas for books and sharings tumble out of me, muses falling over themselves to get through the clogged doorways of my exhausted mind. Characters come to life in the small hours of insomnia, and in the daytime, paintings and drawings give me great joy in the love of vibrancy and colour that is denied me in so many other areas of my life.

Most of all, there is the presence of the Holy Three-in-One, who delights in me despite my weakness. He has taught me that if I am an anchoress like Julian, it is to him that I am tethered, like a tree whose roots are forever wrapped around the solidness of rock beneath. He has assured me too, that despite the smallness of my cell, it is teaching me everything, as the desert mothers and fathers knew it would. Also, that there is some small light shining out of the windows here to help guide others either towards God and/or away from the possibility of wrecking rocks. Given the state of my life I suspect I am more likely a horrible warning than a good example! But then, it is his light that is radiating from me, and in spite of me.

The lighthouse is an image we come back to over and over again, God and I. I share it with you here in hopes that those of you who are trapped in difficult or trying circumstances might garner some hope. However small or difficult our lives are, however tiny our sphere of existence, God can and will be with us wherever we find ourselves. He will make himself known through love, truth and his merciful, beautiful grace, whether we are able to see it or not. Wicked witches may do their worst, confining us to inescapable circumstances, but they cannot ever stop the light of his love from shining.

Keren Dibbens-Wyatt is a chronically ill writer and artist with a passion for poetry, mysticism, story and colour. Her writing features regularly on spiritual blogs and in literary journals. She is the author of the book Recital of Love (Paraclete Press 2020), lives in South East England and is mainly housebound by her illness.

The Light of Life Shines Into the Darkness of Death

by Catherine Lawton

Memories and conflicting emotions arise at Christmas time. Even the first Christmas was full of contrasts. Humble shepherds preceded regal wisemen. A brilliant star illumined a crude manger. Memories of joys as well as sorrows are intensified during the holidays.

What a joyous Christmas it was the year I brought my first child home from the hospital on Christmas Eve. In our tiny house, my husband had hung blinking lights on the fresh-cut fir tree. In the darkness, I held the baby and watched the colored lights dancing and reflecting on the ceiling. I was awed by the mystery and sacredness of life. I could almost hear the angels singing and the heavenly bells ringing. I thought of Mary. Did she sense the same holy presence as she held her newborn and gazed into the night sky at the display of heavenly light?

My son's Christmas birth awakened in me a sense of wonder at the miracle of life and God's love. To think that another baby had been born 2,000 years ago who embodied the eternal, holy God! Through His birth Jesus entered human existence. Through His death, we may enter His eternal, exalted existence. Mary couldn't know that it was Jesus' victory in death as well as in life that brought such joy in the heavens and caused his birth to be celebrated for centuries afterward.

Then there was the Christmas that my mother died. With her music and baking and decorating, she had always made Christmas celebrations special. She loved life and didn't want to die while still in her forties. But as cancer ravaged and finally took her, she departed with a smile on her face. I could almost hear the angels singing and the heavenly bells ringing. And I thought of Mary again. As she watched Jesus die a tragic, painful death, did she despair? Or did the memory of the miracles surrounding his birth and life give her hope? Life won out. His death brought our spiritual birth.

122

In the pain of death's separation, in my heart was born an awareness of the vitality of Christmas that I will carry with me forever. With my family, I stood in the snow at Mother's hillside grave. I looked up and noticed the first twinkle of an evening star. Our hope still shone! The realities of pain, suffering, and death are inescapable. But they will end in miraculous everlasting life because of the shining hope of Christmas.

So now as we draw into our warm lungs the chill air and watch the lights--like stars--twinkle, we can smile through our tears and celebrate the memories and the hope of Christmas!

Catherine Lawton has authored several books including a biblical novel and two collections of poetry. Inner healing is a theme running through her writing, as she explores the depths of our relationships with—and need for—God, nature, and each other. Cathy is editor in chief at Cladach Publishing: https://cladach.com/catherine-lawton/.

The Light of Christ

by Rodney Marsh

John tells us that all of creation "received its life" from God and God gave "light to everyone" with the gift of life (Jn 1:3,4 The Message). No exceptions — no time, place or person in all creation has been, or will be, without the light of God. God's promise is that darkness will never eliminate God's light from God's world.

There is parable of the light and life of God in the June 2018 Thai cave rescue of twelve Thai Soccer boys who had become trapped in a dark, flooded cave. After twelve days of searching for them, hope of rescue was fading. Yet God's light and life was with and within the boys and their coach, Ekkapol Chantawong (Ek). It was God's light and life that enabled Ek to show the boys a path through this time of dark isolation. Following the death of his father, Ek became an orphan and between the ages of ten and twenty, Ek had been raised in a Buddhist monastery. Before leaving the monastry, Ek received training as a novice monk. This training for Ek was a vital source of his capacity to care for and encourage the boys during the dark days and nights, waiting for rescue. Ek's fatherly guidance was the reason the boys' situation did not descend into a "Lord of the Flies" scenario. God's light in Ek enabled him to teach the boys to settle, meditate and discover the light within them instead of allowing their minds to be trapped by fears prompted by their dire circumstances.

The "Wild Boars" boys and their coach reminds us that God's light is always searching for incarnation in our darkness. We learn that just as God's light found embodiment in Ek and the boys, it will find embodiment in you and in me in our darkest times and God's light will enable us to communicate hope to others in our common darkness. John emphasised that God's embodied "light keeps shining" at all times and no darkness has been, or ever will be, able to extinguish God's light of love. This persistence of the light was shown in the rescue of the boys.

To be rescued, the Wild Boars boys and their coach needed rescuers. The story of their rescue contains another analogy to the coming of the light of Christ into our world. As John says of Jesus, "The true light that gives light to everyone was coming into the world," (Jn 1:9) and the light of rescue was coming for Ek and the boys. After twelve days and nights of blackness, like the shepherds on a hill long ago, a frightening light shattered the boys' darkness. In oft repeated TV footage, we saw the befuddled boys being blinded by the bright lights of the British divers who found them. It was different for the shepherds at Jesus' birth. Though the light shone on the shepherds, they could see into the light but the boys were temporarily blinded by the light. As in modern campouts when mutually blinding LED head torches (head lamps) mean we see neither who is looking at us nor who we are looking at. The boys were blinded by the light so they needed to hear their rescuer's words of reassurance. They had been found!

The rescue of the boys, however, had only just begun. How were they to be brought out alive from the cave? The rescue was eventually led by Adelaide anaesthetist and expert cave diver, Dr "Harry" Harris and his dive partner, Dr Craig Challen (a veterinarian) from Perth. They were called to help by the British team of divers who found the boys. The British divers knew Harry and Craig were uniquely qualified and experienced in the physical and medical aspects of a difficult cave rescue. Later, Harry admitted thinking, at the time, that there was only a small possibility of getting all the boys out alive. Each boy was sedated and one by one they were accompanied and guided by Thai divers out of the cave. Harry was the last to emerge. Harry and Craig had spent over seventy hours in the cave. After the boys had all reached safety alive, "Speaking to Prime Minister Malcolm Turnbull via FaceTime, Dr Harris said the 'big heroes' were the twelve boys themselves, and the Thai Navy SEAL divers who looked after them in the cave."[37]. What a beautiful story of the light of compassion reaching into our dark world. Harry, however, paid a price for his involvement in the rescue, because shortly after he emerged from the cave, he was informed his father had died whilst he was on the rescue mission.

When Harry received the call to assist he knew his father was ill and he faced a choice whether or not to take part in the rescue. He chose to help. We, too, daily make choices about what kind of person we are to be in God's world. Are we choosing each day to be a light bringer? Harry's boss said of him ,"Harry is a quiet and kind man who did not think twice about offering his support on this mission." Just so Jesus, who "gave up everything and became a slave, when he became like one of us." Jesus, our Rescuer, "has delivered us from the domain of darkness and transferred us to the kingdom of his beloved Son" (Col. 1:13 ESV). Each day we can show we are in the light by ourselves becoming an embodiment of the light of love for those with whom we live and work.

The message of Christmas is that the love of God is always seeking embodiment. The light of God's love found complete embodiment in Jesus. Now Jesus names his followers as 'the light of the world'. Paul also tells Jesus' followers at Ephesus "you were darkness, but now… you are light" (Eph 5:8). Jesus followers are not only in the light but are light in the Lord. God's eternal love and light are always seeking embodiment in God's world and Advent asks us the question: *Are you bringing the light of God's love into this world of darkness?*

Prayer: Lord, you tell me, I am light in you. Today and every day grant me the gift of the Spirit of your Son to be light in the dark places I will encounter this day. Amen.

Rodney is a retired Minister of the Word in the Uniting Church in Australia having served as a Parish Minister, teacher and school Chaplain in South Western Australia. Rodney enjoys swimming, gardening and retains an interest in Biblical Studies, meditation and reconciliation with the traditional owners of the land.

Into the Light

by Lynn Domina

I see their photos nearly daily without ever fully believing the images. I've heard testimony from friends and neighbors and recently even my own daughter. In the deep hours of night, especially as autumn is turning toward winter, northern lights ignite the sky. I've never seen them. I used to assume I never would, for they hold such a special mystical significance—something I believe is true, even trust is true, yet now can't possibly be true. Their beauty is too strange.

I live now along the shore of Lake Superior, which always looks majestic, whether the day is calm or stormy or the sky above it is clear or dark with clouds. I gaze at the lake, resting in its expanse, and then I look up toward the sky, measuring the boundary between water and air. I live now far enough north that at the winter solstice, we'll see just over eight and a half hours of daylight. I'll leave for work in darkness and arrive home in darkness. I wouldn't want to spend my entire life walking through the dark, but at least for now, such short days still seem exotic. And I know that late one night, maybe next month or maybe next year, I'll step outside, and there they'll be, the aurora borealis, northern lights, shimmering waves of green or purple or blue. I won't believe it.

In this season of short days, I'm waiting for the stretched out light of spring, but even more, I'm hoping to see the glorious undulations of the northern lights. I'll be grateful for both. The feeling is different, responding to the ordinary and the extraordinary. During the long days and the short days, I feel contentment, each day unfolding as it should. When I do see the northern lights, I expect to feel awe, as creation reveals itself to be even more astonishing than I could have imagined.

My response to the light I experience and the lights I hope to see mirrors my understanding of faith. I wander through my days, occasionally perceiving the ordinary grace that envelopes me, grace that is always more than enough to make this life meaningful. I wake up next to my spouse and watch her breathing, and then I hear my

127

daughter rumbling around in her room. I step out onto the sidewalk and see the clouds reflecting dawn. I taste the grilled cheese I've made for my lunch, knowing that it nourishes my body as much as it satisfies my spirit. I attend a poetry reading and hear another person creating art through language, dedicating her life to observation and testimony and self-expression. I receive each of these moments as a blessing, knowing that they're mine because God first created this world and then brought me into it. These moments are as ordinary as the days that lengthen and then contract, and they are enough to make me glad for this life.

And yet, my faith also tells me there's more, even if I haven't yet experienced it directly. My faith confirms that the God who created each of us also became incarnated to share our human experiences and continues to sustain us. Being alive in this world is enough. But my faith teaches me that my indirect experiences of God will one day become direct. The light I walk within every ordinary day will blaze across the night sky like nothing I've ever seen before. Walking in the light, walking toward the light, walking through the night and waiting for it to flare with color makes life itself an Advent experience. I wait expectantly, aware that my ordinary life and its extraordinary moments reveal the God who also waits, expectantly, filled with hope, exuding light.

Lynn Domina's latest book is Devotions from HERstory: 31 Days with Women of Faith. She serves as Head of the English Department at Northern Michigan University and as Creative Writing Editor of The Other Journal. You can read more here: www.lynndomina.com.

Leaning into the Light

by Ellen Haroutunian

Our church has a tradition of creating an Advent "waiting room" which is simply our church courtyard lit with white mini bulbs. The light is soft and dim, and the air is cold. We shiver together and sip hot chocolate as we wait to be invited inside. Last Sunday evening, I distinctly remember thinking that what made this cold and dark wait tolerable, even enjoyable, was sharing it with friends as we recalled our week's journeys, and teased and chatted. But waiting is rarely so easy.

Those simple memories of moments shared became a warm wrap of assurance for what was to come. When I first wrote this, what had followed was two mass shootings, one in Georgia and then in San Bernardino. That year there were more mass shootings (defined by 3 or more victims) than there were days in the year. That was one of the darkest and coldest Advents I could remember. Looking back now from 2020, few of us could have imagined how much more fragmented and polarized the nation would become.

I had had a pretty Advent blog post all ready to go. But I felt despondent and angry. The senseless and violent loss of life was abhorrent enough, but that last heartbreaking shooting seemed to only serve to polarize people even more than ever. Many seemed to entrench themselves more deeply into their ideologies, wearing them like bulletproof vests as if they had the power to save. Most disturbingly, the resoluteness of what has absorbed so much of American Christianity today—this civil, nationalistic religion that is so often diametrically opposed to the ways of Jesus—seems to have become more unyielding.

I resonate with Karl Rahner's cry,

"You were supposed to redeem us from ourselves and yet you, who alone are absolutely free and unbounded, were 'made' even as we are. Of course I know that you remained what you always were, but still, didn't our mortality make you shudder, you the Immortal God? Didn't you, the broad and limitless Being, shrink back in horror from our narrowness? Weren't you, absolute Truth, revolted at our pretense?"[38]

I am deeply saddened, even revolted by it.

There's a significant part of American "Christianity" that has lost its way. It has shrunken its identity to being defined by an orthodoxy test. One can say they believe in Jesus Christ the Son of God, and that he was crucified and raised from the dead, and then live as if that great love has no further bearing on our lives. Gone is the deep and ancient sense of the sacramental nature of everything. "Am I my brother's keeper?" (Gen. 4:9), they cry.

The way of Jesus has been forgotten.

In a culture where his own brethren were oppressed by the violence and power of the Roman Empire, Jesus taught the mystifying way of peace.

He taught a way that did not seek rights or power. Nor did he need weapons to feel safe or to intimidate others. His implements were the tools of a servant: a basin and towel.

American "Christianity" applauds spending more than half the federal budget on war machine, but strains at gnats: the relatively small amounts of money needed for food stamps, safety nets, and health care subsidies. We turn our backs on the poor and hungry.

The US spends more on its military budget than 10 other nations combined, and that includes Russia and China. Power is seen as a godly virtue. There is a profound fear of loss of safety, control, and a preferred lifestyle and its sensibilities. But Jesus's paradoxical view of power is the kenotic path, the laying down of all claims to power and rights. Jesus's way is strange and even dangerous in a world like this. Yet he says, "Follow me."

American "Christianity" has forgotten how to see God in our midst.
In a culture where the highly religious could easily pass by a wounded man in the road, Jesus applauded the love of an outsider—a Samaritan —for his genuine care for him. Now, that wounded man on the road is actually the frightened, traumatized young children separated from their parents at our border. He is the hungry children whose parents' unemployment benefits just ran out. He is the black woman who was

shot to death in her sleep by those sworn to protect her. He is Jesus himself. Once again it is not the self-identified religious "in" group but the "Samaritans" who are trying to advocate for them. "Samaritans," whom American "Christianity" does not recognize as being part of their faith.

American "Christianity" defines itself by who is allowed in and who is not.

In a culture where only those who were deemed ceremonially clean by religious leaders could enter the temple and worship God, Jesus touched a bleeding women, healed those deemed unclean by disease, welcomed the sinners and ate and drank with them. Jesus seems to let just anyone in. He has very low standards.

American "Christianity" wants to withhold healthcare from those who have not earned it or do not deserve in their eyes.

In a culture where the high religious scoffed at the poor openly, Jesus showed no preference for the "deserving poor." He fed the hungry and healed the sick. He did not check to see if they were worthy or deserving. The god of Mammon has blinded us to what is truly important—Jesus warned us about the god that sees only scarcity even as it grabs as much as it can for itself. Jesus showed us that there is no scarcity in God.

American "Christianity" has turned its back on the refugee who is fleeing unspeakable violence due to political and military unrest in his homeland. Like Jesus, the refugee has nowhere to lay his head.

In a culture where strict adherence to the practices of the religious law could bring power and honor,
Jesus made it clear that what we do to the least of these—the suffering one, the hungry and thirsty one, the outcast and stranger, is what we do to him. American "Christianity" has turned him away.

American "Christianity" preaches pro-life that is not pro-life.

This is the watershed issue. Yet other western nations with safe and legal abortion have much lower rates of abortion than we do, without invoking legislative power over a woman's bodily integrity. Briefly, it is because the vast majority of abortions are due to financial reasons and they have chosen to care for lower income people and the poor. They make birth control and health education affordable and easily accessible.

Conversely, desperate women will go underground. There is a thriving abortion industry in the places where it is illegal. But to challenge the god of Mammon and care for those who struggle financially does not rally a voting bloc nor does it create the righteous outrage that cements group cohesion. In truth, it cares little about unborn lives. And with the hyper-focus on this one issue, the struggles of black lives, Native lives, immigrant lives, female lives, the lives of all marginalized groups, are simply not seen.

American "Christianity" has become an allegiance to dogma and behavior that makes us feel upright and safe. It circles the wagons of loyalty around us. Tragically, it also protects us from God and all that the Kingdom asks of us. We remain safely unchanged.

So while waiting outside in the cold, aching to get inside, aching for things to be made right, I hear the Advent story ask, "Do you see?" "Advent is, above all else, a call to full consciousness…", says Richard Rohr[39]. It is meant to wake us up. Jesus has brought a new way of being in this world. Jesus *is* the way.

Indeed, in this time of waiting, we can attune to the profound ache of the world, represented by a poor family who had to flee for their very lives from a violent ruler. May it be a startling and wondrous wake up call. Many are beginning to see that this civic, nationalistic religion is not the way of Jesus. Many are weary of a religiosity that marginalizes the poor and less advantaged, that cares little for the plight of the refugee and stranger, and has what Ben Corey calls a "sadistic fetish" with guns. Many are waking up and seeing that we have exchanged the truth of the Good News for the lie of a civic religion and a good life. Many are awakening to a longing for true Shalom, peace on earth. Shalom does not eliminate others to find peace, Shalom is created in the peace among "others."

Rahner continues,

> "Slowly a light is beginning to dawn. I have begun to understand what I have known for a long time. You are still in the process of your coming…. It is said that you will come again and this is true. But the word again is misleading. It won't really be another coming, because you have never really

gone away. In the human existence that you made your own for all eternity, you have never left us."[40]

We wait for the Light to come, and yet the Light is already here.

Advent allows us to reexamine our own ache that longs for the coming of God in our midst, not just for ourselves, but also for the flourishing of all. Advent opens up a space in us to receive God who is *not* revolted by our narrowness and pretense, but who is pleased to be with us, as us, as we are. It opens our eyes to see God-with-us. It can even open up a space in me for *them*, lest I cast them out as they have cast me out. In this time when so much of Christianity has lost the plot, Advent is opportunity for us all to begin anew. Then, like Jesus, we can dive right into the world with only faith, hope and love as our accoutrements. We can believe again that God's love will always have the last word.

Welcome Advent, welcome Christmas. May the Christ, the God who loves in flesh and bone, right here, right now, be birthed in us this season.

Ellen Haroutunian is a Spiritual Director, psychotherapist, life coach, writer, and a doctoral student focusing on spiritual formation and contemplative practices. She has two grown children and lives in Lakewood, CO with her husband Aram, two ex-racing greyhounds, and two non-racing cats. She is a pot stirrer, a world changer, and occasionally dons a T-Rex suit.

Blue Christmas? Or Christmas of Hope? – December 22

by Barbie Perks

Close on twenty years ago, I came across the Blue Christmas concept in a Methodist Women's magazine that was being published in South Africa. The idea resonated deeply as we had suffered a number of losses that year in our church community: deaths, divorces, jobs and relationships. I contacted our pastor and suggested we hold a service the week before Christmas to recognise the losses in our community and he agreed, with the proviso that I organise it! I am always grateful to him for the trust and confidence he had in me as a person, and that service birthed what is now an integral part of the church's Christmas calendar.

After that first service, we renamed it our Christmas of Hope service, a time when we can focus on caring for those who have suffered loss in any way, recognise the brokenness that grief brings, and give them hope to face the future, confident of the support of the church community, and with the knowledge that Christ is with them in all aspects of their lives. The liturgy, combined with an invitation to come forward to light a candle in remembrance of what we have lost, is particularly comforting to many.

What we need most when life is at its darkest point, is that flicker of light, that hope that things will eventually get better. Sometimes it takes a long time, but when we hold on to Christ as our anchor through it all, God makes a way and we can move forward.

I returned to my home church for a visit last week, and was reminded of this service again, and how poignant it is for me as I am now the one walking this road of uncertainty. This Christmas will be a very different one, in a different home, in a different country, among different friends. Thankfully, some family members will be joining us and I am sure it will be a wonderful week. The amazing truth of it all, is that no matter the where, the why and the how, the retelling of the birth of our Saviour is a constant source of comfort and hope.

A favourite Christmas carol is "We Three Kings" — we sing of the star and the light that leads us, and there are times when that light is literally all we have to hang onto in the darkness of grief and sorrow.

Two songs I found online that are very meaningful are played by The Piano Guys[41] and Casting Crowns[42].

I'm updating this post because I know that Christmas 2020 is going to be a very different and extremely difficult Christmas time for a lot of us. There has been so much fear, isolation, illness, death, political, emotional and economic instability in the entire world as a result of the Covid-19 pandemic — can we even begin to imagine a normal / usual Christmas time? What new insights will we receive when we read the story of the birth of Christ again? How will God use this time to draw us closer to Him?

The liturgy for the candle lighting is very meaningful — maybe you would like to create your own advent candle wreath, and use the following liturgy for your own celebration.

May the Lord of Peace grant you peace this advent season — may He inhabit your praises, and bring you joy.[43]

Barbie Perks has been married to Mike for thirty-six years, and has two adult sons, a grandson of three and a granddaughter of one. She and Mike currently live in Tanzania where they are involved in a small international Christian fellowship. Adapting to a small community has been interesting in many ways. God is at work everywhere they go!

Christmas Eve and
Christmas through Epiphany

The Mood of Christmas by Howard Thurman

Today's poems are by African American theologian Howard Thurman (November 18, 1899 – April 10, 1981) an influential American author, philosopher, theologian, educator and civil rights leader. He was Dean of Chapel at Howard University and Boston University for more than two decades, wrote 21 books, and in 1944 Thurman cofounded San Francisco's Church for the Fellowship of All Peoples, the first integrated, interfaith religious congregation in the United States. They are from the book, The Mood of Christmas and Other Celebrations.

"The Work of Christmas"
When the song of the angels is stilled,
When the star in the sky is gone,
When the kings and princes are home,
When the shepherds are back with their flock,
The work of Christmas begins:
To find the lost,
To heal the broken,
To feed the hungry,
To release the prisoner,
To rebuild the nations,
To bring peace among people,
To make music in the heart.

"Christmas Is Waiting to be Born"
Where refugees seek deliverance that never comes
And the heart consumes itself as if it would live,
Where children age before their time
And life wears down the edges of the mind,
Where the old man sits with mind grown cold,
While bones and sinew, blood and cell, go slowly down to death,
Where fear companions each day's life,
And Perfect Love seems long delayed.
CHRISTMAS IS WAITING TO BE BORN:
In you, in me, in all mankind.[44]

When the Longest Night Never Seems to End - December 23

by Kathie Hempel

I remember Christmas' Eves long ago when my sons were very young. Not always fondly.

As a single Mom, with no close family of my own, it was a struggle that I always felt I lost. I wanted to be able to see the boys' faces on Christmas morning. I had worked hard to be able to afford at least one thing they really wanted Santa to bring. It just wasn't enough.

I would imagine that moment they opened the presents and saw they had gotten exactly what they wanted from the Sears Toy Catalog…but then what? What would we do with the other fifteen and a half hours of the day?

Sure, I could cook a nice dinner. The four of us could sit around the kitchen table, however, I could not imagine it would feel like Christmas.

Then, I would think of their Dad's family. All the aunts and uncles and cousins, grandma and grandpa, the noise of everyone talking and singing carols and comparing gifts. I could not compete with that. And so, each year, regardless of shared custody and the swapping of turns with the children during the holiday, I would pack up their little overnight bags and send them off with their presents for others and wish them the merriest of Christmas'.

Many times, I would collapse against the door after it closed behind them and sob. All I wanted to do was to crawl into bed and sleep until it was over. Just waiting for it to end. Was that all that Christmas had come to mean to me? How I wished for something different!

Today, I look back on those days quite differently. I hope my boys remember Christmas as a happy time. I believe they can, based on all the wonderful stories and laughter that came home from those

139

Christmas' that were spent with Dad and his family. And I smile, knowing I did the best thing I could for them at the time.

When Christmas doesn't seem as merry as the televisions commercials tell us it should be, perhaps it is time to look back on that first Christmas Eve. There were no sparkling trees or brightly covered gifts. Just a young man and woman, looking down at a baby they had not conceived together, and yet, would raise as their own. They were shunned by many they knew and amazed by the remarkable happenings that followed a message from an angel. And now, here he was.

He looks so... human. They wonder how exactly does one raise the human son of a Divine God? Shepherds and wise men, angels on high, murder in a King's heart. There must have been times this very human couple wished for something different.

Yet, based on the hope of the prophets and the voice of the angel, they moved forward. It had to be backbone, not wishbone, that would allow them to complete the extraordinary mission ahead.

Luke 2:19 says: "But Mary treasured up all these things and pondered them in her heart." Is it possible that the secret to our survival of the most difficult times of our lives is contained in this one short verse?

Here is a mother, who counted hope as treasure. How often did she think of all the events that led to that moment? How often did she have to remember, in wonder, the promises of the angel?

Her son was not always easy to understand. He disappeared while they were traveling, it took them three days to find the boy and when they did, he was not exactly apologetic. "'Why were you searching for me?' he asked. 'Didn't you know I had to be in my Father's house?'" But they did not understand what he was saying to them, according to Luke 2:41-52 and again "... his mother treasured all these things in her heart."

During a wedding, she asks for a favor and Jesus at first seems hesitant, she goes to visit him surrounded by crowds of strangers and He asks "who is my mother?" (Mt 12:48). I would not be pleased!

Mary's toughest time of all comes at the foot of a cross, with mockers tossing lots for her son's clothes, watching soldiers stab him and offering him vinegar when he desperately needs water. He tells a friend to watch over her and then says, "it is finished" (Jn 19:30).

Finished? How could that be? An angel said he was going to save the world! That he was a King! She had gone through so much!

These were not, I am quite sure the dreams she had for her babe in the manger. And yet, when the day of Pentecost arrives, we find Mary praying with the disciples. Her dreams did not materialize as she had wished, however, her hope obviously persevered.

Hope is what was given that first Christmas. Hope is what sustains us in the tough times, during the longest of long and lonely nights. In hope, we remember that the times when the end seems nearest, there is yet the promise of new beginnings.

When the night seems too long, we need to treasure this hope in our hearts and think on these things.

[11] For I know the plans I have for you," declares the Lord, "plans to prosper you and not to harm you, plans to give you hope and a future. [12] Then you will call on me and come and pray to me, and I will listen to you. [13] You will seek me and find me when you seek me with all your heart (Jer 29:11-13).

Kathie Hempel is a freelance writer living in Dundas, Ontario, Canada with her husband Phil and two Bichon dogs, Bailey and Muggles.

Anticipation and Reality: A Christmas Reversal - Christmas Eve

by Rev Jeannie Kendall

Anticipation is a curious thing: and perhaps especially at Christmas. As a child, my favourite part of Christmas was Christmas Eve. I loved the colours of the presents under the tree, and the mystery of which ones were for who and what they might contain within. If I am ruthlessly honest about those far off days though, often the expectation outshone the reality and I enjoyed the thought of what might be rather than what actually was. My parents made us open presents one at a time each day, eking them out until well past New Year. I never minded, because it lengthened that season of hope of what I might discover hiding under the gaudy exterior.

Sometimes life is like that, with the anticipation superior to the actuality. The holiday which we eagerly await but weather or venue disappoint us. The job we hoped would stretch and develop us which turns out to be monotonously mundane. The friendship from which we hoped more but proved ultimately superficial.

There are many different ways we can respond. We can stop hoping, allowing spider threads of disillusionment to wrap themselves around our soul. Or we can become weary in the waiting, continuing to yearn for that moment which will surprise us by finally meeting our unspoken dreams. As the Bible puts it, "Unrelenting disappointment leaves you heartsick" (Proverbs 13:12, The Message).

Christmas, it seems to me, is the opposite. At the time of Jesus' birth, after a 400-year silence from God, surely anticipation had either ceased altogether or been retained only by the pious few. And those who hung on had only nationalistic expectations: a warrior Messiah who would crush the Roman oppressors and release the browbeaten Israelites.

Yet, the actuality was so much greater. A rescuer not just for the Jews and that limited time, but for every nation and all history and bringing ultimate transformation for the cosmos. Love personified, humanity dignified and restored.

So, as Christmas Eve melts into Christmas Day, whatever the day itself holds, know that, to quote the next half of that verse from Proverbs, "a desire fulfilled, it is a tree of life" (Prov 13:12 NRSV). An apt phrase, as, decades later, that tree of death would give us access to full, free, technicolour life.

For once, as we remember again the Word becoming flesh, the reality far exceeds every expectation.

Jeannie Kendall works freelance writing and teaching. She lives in Surrey with her husband and has two grown up children and 2 grandchildren. Her first book, Finding Our Voice, was published by Authentic Media in 2019 and her second, on the subject of tears, is due out in 2021. Her website is www.jeanniekendall.co.uk

Christmas in our Imaginations - Christmas Day

by Andy Wade

I wonder what it was really like, that day the Prince of Peace was born. Mary and Joseph must have been churning with emotion. As new parents, there would have been joy and amazement as this delicate child emerged from the womb and gave out his first cry.

In the back of their minds though, what must they have been thinking? They had received those strange messages from God about this baby, and Joseph knew he was not the natural father. I imagine their joy was mixed with large portions of wonder, fear, anticipation, and confusion. How could they begin to take it all in?

Then the shepherds arrived with their unbelievable story about a host of angels announcing to them the birth of Mary and Joseph's little child. Mary "pondered" all these things in her heart. What a tame word for all the swirling emotions she must have been experiencing!

We all have images of these events in our minds. From years of stories, Christmas pageants, and carols, our ideas of Jesus' birth have been shaped. We have images of "three kings" journeying from the East to worship the newborn King of the Jews, yet the number of Magi is never mentioned. Similarly, our minds may conjure images of Mary and Joseph turned away from some kind of local hotel, finding shelter in a barn or a cave with the animals.

But the words used to describe the "inn" actually refer to a kind of upper family room, a guest room, that was already full, so they had to stay in the lower part of the home where the animals were brought in during the evening. It's highly unlikely that they were alone in the room. Mary was almost certainly attended to by various female family members as she gave birth. (For more see *Jesus Through Middle Eastern Eyes* by Kenneth E. Bailey.)

The power of story can shape our understanding of the birth of Jesus. More often than not these pretty stories downplay the radical nature of what God was up to in this miraculous birth.

We know the shepherds were there, welcomed into the room with Jesus. We've heard how radical it was for these shepherds to be

144

present, to be the first to hear the Good News. But I also wonder what it must have been like for Joseph's extended family. They also were required to journey to Bethlehem for the census.

- What must have been going through their minds?
- Was this all still a disgrace for the family, or had they somehow reconciled themselves to the scandal?
- Were Mary and Joseph staying with family there, or had they been shunned?
- If you were one of the extended family there for the census, how would you get your head around the news from the shepherds? Could you accept it?

We don't know the answers to these questions; all we can do is guess. We don't even know if Joseph's parents were still alive. But what if they were? Can you imagine what it would be like to be Joseph's father in this situation? What would you be feeling if you were Joseph's mother? Was the scandal made more palatable because their social status was already rather low? Did they hold onto family, in spite of the embarrassment, embracing this child as one of their own?

I wonder…

Was this Jesus' first act of reconciliation, of "drawing all things to himself" (Jn 12:32), to bring this family which had been fractured by scandal, back together? Or was this instead part of the fulfillment of Jesus' more difficult words:

> "Do you think I came to bring peace on earth? No, I tell you, but division. From now on there will be five in one family divided against each other, three against two and two against three. They will be divided, father against son and son against father, mother against daughter and daughter against mother, mother-in-law against daughter-in-law and daughter-in-law against mother-in-law" (Lk 12:51-53).

With Mary, I ponder. Filled with wonder and awe, with anticipation tinged with confusion, I ponder.

As we live into our faith as best we can, the flaws in our own assumptions are revealed. We wrestle, knowing in whom we trust, in whom we believe, yet also aware how often this same faith, "we don't yet see things clearly. We're squinting in a fog, peering through a mist." (1 Cor. 13:12 The Message), has manifested with both love and hate, reconciliation and division, hope and despair.

Even as we celebrate Emmanuel, God-with-us, we're stuck admitting we don't have all the answers, and some of the "answers" we have are more problematic than helpful. Yet we continue to believe,

to wrestle,

to hope,

to sit in wonder, and ponder all these things in our hearts.

For to us a child is born,
to us a son is given,
and the government will be on his shoulders.
And he will be called
Wonderful Counselor, Mighty God,
Everlasting Father, Prince of Peace.

(Isa. 9:6)

Andy Wade is the facilitator for M25 the Gorge focusing on immigrant/ immigration issues and walking with our Latinx neighbors. He serves on the Gorge Ecumenical Ministries board and lives in Hood River, OR with his wife, Susan.

A Glimpse of Glory - December 26

by Keren Dibbens-Wyatt

I have been revisiting some of the books that enchanted me as a young girl, ostensibly as research for my own writing, but in fact more truly because in my middle age, I am hankering for the simpler joys. Having read all the Anne of Green Gables books my county library had to offer (I should be receiving the next one today if my husband took any notice of my Christmas list). I started on another series written by the same wonderful Canadian author, Lucy Maud Montgomery, about Emily of New Moon.

Emily is a little girl with a sensitive soul, and every so often, she senses something she calls "the flash." It is a glimpse into eternity, into the essence of beauty, and it comes unbidden at various moments:

> It always seemed to Emily… that she was very, very near to a world of wonderful beauty. Between it and herself hung only a thin curtain; she could never draw the curtain aside — but sometimes, just for a moment, a wind fluttered it, and then it was as if she caught a glimpse of the enchanting realm beyond — only a glimpse- and heard a note of unearthly music…. It had come with a high, wild note of wind in the night, with a shadow-wave over a ripe field… with the singing of "Holy, holy, holy," in church, with a glimpse of the kitchen fire when she had come home on a dark autumn night, with the spirit-like blue of ice palms on a twilit pane, with a felicitous new word when she was writing down a "description" of something. And always when the flash came to her, Emily felt that life was a wonderful, mysterious thing of persistent beauty.[45]

Montgomery is a wonderful writer with a great gift for vivid "descriptions" herself, and for delicious characterisation and dialogue. In Emily's ability, she has captured, for me, something about the existence of holy magic; that truly awe-inspiring hint of heaven we can be privy to now and again, as we see a rip in the fabric of the ordinariness of things, or maybe even the divine essence reflected to be almost incarnate in that very ordinariness.

During this season of Advent, we may be looking for a glimpse of where the sacred otherworldly might be found in the hectic and commercialised run up to Christmas. We might be exploring whether it is possible to reclaim the peace and joy only Jesus can give us from the midst of the chaos. I know that we can. More importantly, perhaps, I know that those who don't know the Lord yet can catch that reality that is so much deeper than our existence out of the corner of their eyes, or on the edge of their senses: from hearing a carol; from sitting in a crowded church watching children fluff their angelic lines; from contemplating the glow of a candle.

These "flashes" really do have a chance to shine through at this time of feasting and gifts, because something in us is searching for them. Christmas is when we know we are supposed to find the magic. And all too often, it seems beyond our grasp, and we are disappointed. Santa didn't visit, we think, he never brought me what I really wanted.

But one year, if we are ready and hungry for more than mince pies and turkey, and never mind whether we have been naughty or nice, if there is that moment of wanting something more, we may well be granted a glimpse of the star of wonder, and nothing will ever be the same again.For that wonder is never more obvious to us than at Christmas, when the ordinary and the heavenly coexist with a daring unknown on other feast days. The King of Kings, wrapped up and lying in the livestock's food trough. A weary young unmarried mother, who is also the virgin handmaiden of God, destined to be Queen of heaven. A worried, unsure step-father to God's flesh, skilled woodworker, yet unable to provide decent refuge for his family just when it was needed most, his carefully crafted world turned upside down. A small town lit up by a majestic star, and the brightness of angels, that will soon be grief-stricken by the murderous actions of a jealous Herod.

The glory and the guttural mixed and held together, the curtain fluttering that in thirty-three years will be ripped in two. The contradictions contained in this nativity scene are stretched as far as the east is from the west, and yet, in the centre, right where I might sometimes just catch my breath at a glimpse of its golden beauty caught on the edge of cheap tinsel, is an unearthly sense of wonder, just like the flash in Emily's sight, that cuts through to my very core through all the commercial, plastic nonsense, and shows me the Christ child, and such beautiful, holy mystery, that my heart leaps with the joy of it, deep and fleeting at the same time, in perfect paradox.

Merry Christmas to all, and may God bless us, every one.

Keren Dibbens-Wyatt is a chronically ill writer and artist with a passion for poetry, mysticism, story and colour. Her writing features regularly on spiritual blogs and in literary journals. She is the author of the book Recital of Love (Paraclete Press 2020), lives in South East England and is mainly housebound by her illness.

Darkness to Light - December 27

by James Prescott

I've always struggled with seasonal affective disorder. I need to get up at 6:00 am for work each weekday morning – and it's noticeable that in the summer months, when it's light outside, it's pretty easy to get myself going. In winter, however, the nights are longer, and it's still dark outside when I wake – and I find it tougher to get up.

There's actually science behind this. The sun gives off something called serotonin, which increases our energy levels, and which our body needs, and can even impact our mood. So in summer, we get more of that in the morning (and during the day generally), so it's a lot easier to get up early, and we're less tired, and our mood is brighter.

Recently, I've been struggling with low moods, anxiety, and have had conflicts in my one-on-one relationship with God. Hurt going back decades has been more exposed, God making it very clear He wanted to deal with this.

One area of my life which was bringing anxiety was work. I was struggling with a relationship with an individual at work and there was a lot of tension. I was at home group sharing this with people, and God gave me a revelation. I realised, when I get up to go to work, it's dark. When I get to the underground rail station, it's dark. And on the London Underground, it's dark.

But when I arrive at the station near my work, and walk up the stairs to the outside world, suddenly, light has dawned. I've literally gone from darkness, to light.

And I had a revelation. That no matter how dark the night gets, how long the darkness lasts, that eventually morning always comes. Dawn always breaks. Light always comes back eventually. The dawn begins whilst it's still dark. There's a moment when light begins to slowly permeate through, more and more, until it takes over. Darkness never, ever, lasts forever.

In response to this, in conjunction with my home group leader, I made a decision. I decided that I would be light to those around me. That instead of choosing fear and anger, and to let darkness literally overwhelm me, I would be an agent of the good, of the light.

I have to say, it changed everything. I repeated it to myself every day to begin with. And eventually it sunk into my subconscious. I was less anxious, less moody, less down. It even helped me get up in the morning.

I began to see so much more clearly the metaphor of darkness and light, in my life, and in the world around me. And for some strange reason, I began to feel a sense of hope in the midst of the darkness this world is in right now.

Which brings me to Christmas. Because Christmas is about light in the darkness. In the midst of a dark night, a baby is born to bring hope to the world. In the darkness of the night, wise men see a light leading them toward the hope of the world. Shepherds up at night, are lit the way towards this saviour.

In every way, Jesus is a light in the darkness. The physical, I believe, reflects what's going on in the supernatural. And the fact that the light always comes in the morning, no matter how dark the night, is a symbol, a sign. It's a promise of God made through creation that no matter how dark things get, there will always be a dawn.

There will always be light. There will always be hope.

Jesus is the human representation of that hope. That in a world overwhelmed by fear and darkness, where love, peace and hope seem so distant – there is still, somehow, hope in the midst of it.

That the sun will rise. There will be a new day. Things will get better.

Our job is to trust, to keep faith in the darkness. To be love to the world around us. Indeed, to try and be light in the darkness around us. God has called us all to represent Him to the world, to keep the faith, to keep loving, to keep hoping and acting for a better world.

This Christmas, let us be reminded to never give up hope. And let us be representative of that light to the world.

James Prescott is an author, blogger and host of the Poema Podcast, which explores the spiritual journey, mental health, grief & creativity. His book 'Mosaic of Grace' was published in 2017. James has also written for Huffington Post and Thrive Global. You can find his work at www.jamesprescott.co.uk and his podcast on all podcast platforms.

Holy Innocents - December 28

by Rev. Jeannie Kendall

For some of us, at least, if we are really honest, we would rather ignore the part in the Christmas story about Herod's massacre at Bethlehem. Enough to manage the shock of God's outrageous risk in entrusting the rescue of his world (and universe) to two unknowns — at least one a teenager — and the precarious nature, especially at that time, of childbirth. How do we begin to process the cost not just to God, but to the nameless families in Bethlehem?

It is not just the historical outrages that we shun, however. Aleppo, the Yemen, countless other places where babies and children die at the hands of our violence and greed — our senses and emotions feel assaulted by the horror and so we close down the emerging thoughts and feelings, and shield ourselves further by silencing the TV or skipping sections in the paper. In our perceived helplessness the reaction is understandable. The scale of suffering causes our compassion to implode: if we felt the full pain of it we would, surely, be subsumed with grief?

I have no answer. But I do wonder if it may help us, whether looking back to Herod or out to our world, to remember that this is essentially the story of individuals. Each one is unique, known to God, and loved by him, however different from that it must feel in the maelstrom of pain. Perhaps a little like this…

Grandmother in Bethlehem
I wasn't ready to become a grandmother.
Somehow it signalled so much:
The gradual dwindling of my own youth
Cemented by this one act:
Denial of my own mortality
Somehow eroded by this new title.
But then I saw him
And it all changed.
Tiny toes, first blue
From traumatic delivery

Then glorious pink
And my heart burst
With relief and pride
And deep protectiveness.
A love like no other.
I was holding him
When the soldiers came.
Never had I so cursed
Female weakness.
I tried to hold him,
Screamed as they pushed me aside
Like the has-been I felt.
I would have died to save him.
And now I only wish I could.

Jeannie Kendall works freelance writing and teaching. She lives in Surrey with her husband and has two grown up children and two grandchildren. Her first book, Finding Our Voice, *was published by Authentic Media in 2019 and her second, on the subject of tears, is due out in 2021. Her website is www.jeanniekendall.co.uk*

Was Jesus Really Born in a Stable and Why Does it Matter? - December 29

by Christine Sine

The baby has arrived, but I wonder: *Where did we welcome him to*? Do we really want him taking up residence in our homes or is it easier to relegate him to the stable, to see him as an outsider, not really part of the family? Seeing Jesus in an out of the way place where disreputable people like shepherds can come to worship without us having to worry about them messing up our homes, makes life easy for us. We get that glow that tells us Jesus is here but there is very little commitment required of us.

According to New Testament theologian Kenneth Bailey in his wonderful book, *Jesus Through Middle Eastern Eyes*, Middle Eastern cultures are known for their hospitality and Joseph was coming home with a new wife and an expected first child so there is no way they would have been relegated to the stable. The whole family was gathering, aunts and uncles, cousins and brothers and sisters. All of them coming home. Yes, there was a census that brought them together but in a fun, loving culture like this, it would not have diminished the welcome or the excitement of a homecoming gathering. The expectation of a baby to be born in their midst and then its arrival heralded by angel choirs, would only have increased the excitement.

As Kenneth Bailey explains, the Greek word *katalyma* or *kataluma* translated as "inn" in Luke 2:7, does not mean a commercial building with rooms for travelers. It's a guest space, typically the upper room of a common village home. The family room had an area, usually about four feet lower, for the family donkey, the family cow, and two or three sheep. They are brought in last thing at night and taken out and tied up in the courtyard first thing in the morning. Mangers were dug out of the stone floor of the living room close to the animals.[46]

It was to this simple village home that the shepherds and wise men alike came. Shepherds, despised and regarded as unclean by their society, are visited by angels and invited to join the great home coming celebration that marks the coming of the child who will become the Messiah. That they were welcomed and not turned away from this home is remarkable. This is good news indeed for the outcast and the despised.

Then the wise men come, according to Bailey, rich men on camels, probably from Arabia. And they come not to the city of Jerusalem, where the Jews thought God's glory would shine, but to the child born in a manger around whom there is already a great light. The wise men come to find a new home, a new place of belonging that has beckoned to them across the world. This, too, is remarkable and good news for people of all nations who long for a place to call home.

Bailey tells us that the birth stories of Jesus "de-Zionize" the Messianic traditions. Hopes and expectations for the city of Jerusalem are fulfilled in the birth of the child Jesus.[47]

The new family, the community that will be formed around this child, does not look to the earthly Jerusalem as its home, but to the heavenly Jerusalem which will come down from heaven as a gift of God at the end of history (Rev. 21:1-4). And it is to this home, a place with no more tears, or oppression or starvation that all of us are beckoned by the birth of Christ.

I love this imagery. Even in the birth of Jesus, we are called towards a new family and a new home. There are family and friends and animals. And special invitations by angels for the despised and rejected, and a star to guide the strangers and those who seem far off. The new family and the home envisioned in the birth of Jesus is inclusive of all accept God's invitation.

What will it take for us to really welcome Jesus into our homes this Christmas season? Visualize this baby being born into your family and into your home. How would he be welcomed? Who would be welcomed with him? Who would not be welcomed into the family circle around him?

I am more convinced than ever that it matters a lot where we think Jesus was born, who was with him and how we relate to him. These days when a baby is born, many young couples keep it cloistered away for the first couple of months, afraid that it will be exposed to germs that it has no immunity to. Most parents would certainly not welcome those who came to see Jesus – first the animals and then the homeless shepherds who slept in the fields at night. Who do we exclude from our families because we are afraid they will contaminate us amid the babies in our midst?

On the other hand, I have friends who always leave an empty chair at the dinner table when they hold a festive meal. It is a symbol of the fact that Jesus is the unseen guest at all our meals, the family member who is always present even when we cannot see him. It makes me wonder if, at this time of year, we should set up the manger in the centre of our dining room tables in preparation for the birth of a baby into our families, a constant reminder that Jesus came to be a part of our family and welcome us into God's eternal family.

Christine describes herself as a contemplative activist, passionate gardener, author, and liturgist. She is the founder of Godspace and her most recent book is The Gift of Wonder: Creative Practices for Delighting in God.

Receive the Prince of Peace - December 30

by Lilly Lewin

I love that the season of Christmas really starts on December 25 and runs until Epiphany on January 6 when we celebrate the Light coming to the Gentiles and the arrival of the Magi. It gives us all extra time to consider this Light, the Prince of Peace who comes for all the world.

How are you receiving the Light so far this Christmas? If you are like me, you are still in recovery mode from family festivities and you need more space to reflect on Jesus and all the Incarnation actually means for yourself and our planet.

How are you receiving the Prince of Peace? How do you need to receive Him? Pause. Consider how you can receive his peace today.

Take a few minutes to breathe in the peace of Jesus before you read on. Picture Jesus placing a blanket of peace and protection on your shoulders, surrounding you in his love. What color is the blanket? What's the texture like? How does this blanket make you feel? Breathe in his peace, breathe out any stress or fear you may be carrying in your body. This may take several deep breaths and several minutes to actually sink in. Receive the Prince of Peace.

What does it look like to bring Light and Peace to our broken world today?

Do you know what it really means to be a peacemaker in your neighborhood, in your city, your family, etc?

I know that Jesus says that peacemakers are blessed, but I'm not sure I really know how to live this out well in my everyday world. One of the people who is teaching me more about peacemaking and bringing peace to our world is Jon Huckins[48], the co-founder of the Global Immersion Project. The mission of Global Immersion Project "is training people of faith to engage our divided world in restorative ways".[49] Jon lives in San Diego, CA and crosses the border on a regular basis. He has built friendships with Border Agents, refugees and the people on the ground working in Mexico and the States. Jon leads teams to the border to learn more and listen to real people, to see and hear their stories, not just the sound bites on the news.

Jon posted this on Facebook:

> As we celebrate the birth of a deliverer born in Bethlehem (Palestine) under the weight of violent occupation, I am grateful for my dear Palestinian friends who show us what peace looks like as they follow Jesus under occupation in Bethlehem today. We see you and, in you, we see Jesus.
>
> As we celebrate the selfless courage of a mother, Mary, fleeing violence while seeking safety, hope and welcome, I am grateful for immigrant friends who teach me to trust in the liberating power of Jesus in ways I can hardly imagine. We see you and, in you, we see Jesus.
>
> The Jesus story didn't just happen. It is happening. It isn't only a passive celebration of the past, it is an active participation in God's (and our) future.
>
> May we have the eyes to see Jesus born in and around us everyday. May our seeing disrupt our assumptions of who is "in" and who is "out", uncover our false allegiances to any kingdom other than God's and liberate us to live like the Jesus we talk about.[50]

That's my prayer this Christmas and for the New Year ahead. To have the eyes to see Jesus born in and around me everyday! I want to see Jesus in the people and places I go in my neighborhood. I want to have eyes to see and ears to hear what Jesus hears and see what Jesus sees, not be blind, and not just see what my bias and privilege sees.

I want to BE a peacemaker not just wish for peace! And I want to live in the reality that everyone is welcome at the manger!

Lilly is a worship curator, speaker, author, artist, and founder of thinplaceNASHVILLE, and freerangeworship.com She creates sacred space prayer experiences and leads workshops & retreats across the country and beyond. She writes the freerangefriday blog each week at Godspacelight.com

What's In A Name? – December 31

by Christine Sine

January 1, in the Christian calendar, is not the beginning of a new year. This is the day we celebrate the circumcision of Christ. Since our cultures are more squeamish than those of our ancestors, modern calendars usually list it as the feast of the Holy Name of Jesus. Just like every Jewish boy, Jesus was circumcised and formally named on the eighth day of his life, and so, one week after Christmas, while we are still celebrating the wonder and the joy of the Saviour who came to dwell amongst us, we celebrate this occasion.

In Jesus' day, a name was far more important than it tends to be today. Introducing a person often just about gave you their whole genealogy and, sometimes, even reflected their personality.

Sometimes I wonder, *How did Mary and Joseph's family and the local villagers feel about him being named Jesus?* The name Yeshua in Hebrew is a verbal derivative of "to rescue, to deliver". It was a common name at that time, but it does not seem to have been a family name as reflected in either Mary's or Joseph's genealogy. I wonder if it was an affront to the family's sensibilities. How dare they call this illegitimate son "saviour".

I also wonder what doubts and fears Mary and Joseph brought to that naming day. I can imagine that Simeon's prophecy was a tremendous reassurance to them:

> Sovereign Lord, now let your servant die in peace,
> as you have promised.
> I have seen your salvation,
> which you have prepared for all people.
> He is a light to reveal God to the nations,
> and he is the glory of your people Israel! (Lk 2:29-32)

Anna's prophecy too, even though we do not know her words, must have reinforced this.

As I thought about this, I found myself reflecting on my own name, *Christine*, which means Christ follower. Now it seems appropriate. Today, I see myself first and foremost as a Christ follower; others tell me the same and I think God does, too. But that has not always been the case. Once it would have been the furthest thing from people's minds when they looked at me. I was a difficult, rebellious child who gave my parents and others much grief. Yet, it was obviously a God-chosen name.

What name do you think God calls you by? What doubts do you have about the appropriateness of that name? What are the prophetic voices that remind you of its authenticity? How does this shape what you plan for the next year?

As a celebration of the naming of Jesus, why not get together with a group of friends for a party — always a good way to shake off those post-Christmas blues. Bring a name book with you. Look up the names of each person in your group and discuss their meanings. Have each person share the story of why they were given that name. Then ask the question, *In what ways does your name reflect the call that God has placed on your life?* Some of you may like to consider a new name that reflects what you believe is God's call on your life. One friend of mine changed his name from Bill to Will because he felt it better reflected his desire to use his life "doing the will of God".

Discuss the names of Jesus. Have each person write down the names that they remember as being applied to Jesus in the Scriptures. You might like to have a competition to see who can think of the most names. Or, you could write a poem or song that reflects these names. End your time with a discussion about how you could represent these different aspects of who Jesus can be to those who live around you. Names matter. What we call Jesus matters. If we see him as Lord it can imply a distant and unapproachable God who is unconcerned for human suffering. If we call him servant, we see him down in the dirty places of our world and we want to join him. If we call him companion, we see him as a friend who walks beside us at all times.

What names best depict the Jesus you follow? How do you want to relate to him on a daily basis? Think about this for a few minutes and then if you have time, use the liturgy[51] provided in the endnotes to reflect on.

Christine describes herself as a contemplative activist, passionate gardener, author, and liturgist. She is the founder of Godspace and her most recent book is The Gift of Wonder: Creative Practices for Delighting in God.

101 Affirmations for the New Year - January 1

by Jenneth Graser

Everything we think, has power! Our thoughts create possibilities in our minds and then we act out of those thoughts. Everything we believe is either true or not. And when we believe something that is not true as though it is, we live out of that belief as our reality. We have all experienced the power of our thinking. For example, if bitten by a dog at a young age, we may continue to have anxiety around dogs as an adult believing all dogs to be dangerous or unpredictable, which is not true for all dogs, but certainly feels true if you were the child with such an experience!

Experiences lead to feelings lead to thoughts lead to behaviours. If we become a super sleuth and invite the Holy Spirit into the breadcrumb trail of our feelings and trace back to where they come from, we can experience freedom and healing by inviting his perspective in. Which, in turn, can lead to no more unreasonable fear of dogs!

We are formed intrinsically through our culture, geographical location, family upbringing, educational background and circumstances to name a few. And when things happen to us in life, we form opinions about life based upon those experiences, whether good or bad.

Scripture is filled with the promises and truth of God. And Jesus encourages us to come to him as the Way, the Truth and the Life. So we can renew our minds by refreshing ourselves at the waters of the Living Word. We can open our hearts and minds to transform belief patterns that are not serving us well.

Part of this process of renewing our minds is by declaring or affirming truth over ourselves to shift the negative thought patterns we have, often which, we are not even aware of. It truly is a process of transformation — "be transformed by the renewing of your mind"(Rom. 12:2).

At the beginning of this year, I started journaling and began to write out a list of affirmations to declare into the new year. I share this with you here and encourage you to write out your own list of affirmations and declarations and say these over your life and situation, knowing that as you say them regularly, you are renewing your mind. Use the Bible as a foundation for your declarations.

As we grow in this transforming process, I believe we will experience a shift in our thinking patterns and enter into greater freedom as a result! It is something I wish to embrace and practice. I think the mind needs some good exercise in thinking just the way I feel my body needs exercise to feel good. All a work in progress![52]

~ 101 Affirmations for the New Year ~

1. I live out of perfect peace
2. There is always an option for me
3. I can choose
4. I do not live out of my past
5. I am open to change
6. I tap into the life-giving Spirit
7. I am one with the Father
8. My creativity is expressed
9. I am not held back
10. I can change my mind
11. My perspectives can shift
12. I enter into every opportunity God opens for me
13. I am provided for
14. Abundance is my nature
15. I am a generous person
16. I like to give to others
17. I look after myself well
18. I love being with God
19. Prayer is a great joy to me
20. I hear from God

21. I am created for freedom
22. There is always a way forward
23. I am not perfect and that is OK
24. I embrace myself with unconditional love
25. I am constantly evolving
26. I let go of my clutter
27. I am excited to try new things
28. I respond to the inspiration of the Spirit
29. I hear from God in my dreams
30. I enjoy the simple pleasures of life
31. I live in harmony with others
32. Even my enemies live at peace with me
33. I forgive all past hurt and offenses
34. My mind is clear at all times
35. I hear God's voice and know what to do
36. God is leading me at all times
37. I let my yes be yes, and my no, no
38. God uses every negative as something that can be turned around for my good
39. A miracle is possible in every moment
40. I am a powerful person
41. What I say has value
42. I know when to speak and when to be silent
43. I am comfortable in my body
44. I forgive myself and others with unconditional love
45. I have fabulous ideas
46. I am a good listener
47. I do not compare myself with others
48. My gifts are freely shared
49. My talents have plenty of room for expression
50. I am amply provided for
51. I am protected
52. I thrive and flourish

53. I sleep deeply and well
54. My relationships are a blessing
55. I do not doubt my abilities
56. I am willing to grow
57. I have a teachable spirit
58. I draw deeply from the wells of salvation
59. I drink of the Living Word
60. I love reading the Bible
61. I read the Bible for intimacy not productivity
62. I am treasured by God
63. I do not perform for love
64. I am loved as I am
65. I rest in the goodness of God
66. My life is in God's timing
67. God is able to lead me well
68. I enjoy resting from work
69. I like to make time for silence
70. I make time for nature everyday
71. I listen to music I love
72. I do nothing out of obligation
73. I am not easily manipulated
74. I discern the way forward
75. I am growing in wisdom
76. I make use of resources for spiritual growth
77. I love to encourage others
78. There is more than enough time for all I need to do
79. I am filled with increasing energy and good health
80. I love to laugh loud and joyfully
81. The best is yet to come
82. The past does not determine the future
83. I have a healthy and hope-filled outlook
84. I trust in God's leadership abilities
85. God desires only good for me

86. I am a good parent
87. I do not expect perfection of myself or others
88. I forgive quickly, and dwell in grace
89. I choose forgiveness and release all past resentments
90. I have a wonderful marriage
91. I have a beautiful relationship with my children
92. I am a joyful person
93. Everything I do, flows out of rest
94. I am intrinsically linked into the Vine and receive all I need from God's abundant supply
95. I am open to correction
96. Every door of opportunity opens for me at just the right time
97. I remain calm in challenging situations
98. I listen to my feelings
99. I am close to God
100. God loves me as his very own child
101. I believe the promises of God

Jenneth and Karl, together with their three daughters, live in a seaside village of the Western Cape, South Africa. She shares a spirit of healing and hope through her writings and contemplative music at www.secretplacedevotion.weebly.com

Christmas Been - January 2

by Ana Lisa de Jong

Christmas is for a moment
the veil lifted,
the light of Christ appearing
through the mist.

The bright glow
of a candle briefly lit,
that for a time
illuminates the room.

As a lover's knock upon the door
causes the heart to lift,
so Christmas is the long awaited visit
to which we open our arms.

Christmas is the birth
of the promised child,
whose innocent dependence
draws from us our love.

So that Christmas is
the veil lifted,
the light of Christ appearing
in a crib.

But we must be careful
to not too soon forget,
the one to whose feet we bring
our treasures.

The bright glow
of a candle briefly lit,
might start and stutter,

until it goes out with the wind.

Or the lover's embrace which warms,
depart,
to leave us waiting
and desirous again.

But Christmas that for a moment
lifts the veil,
shows us what lies always
behind the scenes of things.

Christ, in love
found a way to remain,
and has given us back our treasures,
surrendered at his feet.

So that the treasure that is Christ,
can be threaded through our days,
strung from one Christmas to the next,
as glowing lights across the heavens.

Ana Lisa de Jong is a poet from Aotearoa, New Zealand, 'Land of the Long White Cloud'. She is the author of five published poetry collections, and generously gives away smaller collections to readers online. Read more: www.livingtreepoetry.com.

Redeeming Time & How to Wait - January 3

by Faith Eury Cho

I never go to the gym during this time of year, because it teems with motivated people who decided to become fitter, skinnier, and healthier as their new year's resolutions. Something about the New Year really spikes people's hope for change, for breakthrough. But by February, that hope tends to dwindle. Perhaps it's because people eventually realize that altering the digits on the calendar does not necessarily hasten change.

Waiting for change, no matter how long the wait, can be such an arduous journey. There are some aspects of change you can control, such as weight loss or personal discipline. However, there are some things that are left in the air, leaving you at God's mercy for when things will shift in your favor. Healing from long-term ailments. Salvation of loved ones. Mounting hospital bills. Unbearable work conditions. You need God to handle these thing because your own strength and will are finite.

Yes, it's true. Your own human efforts, as mighty as they may be, are incomparable to the infinitely powerful hand of God. You can manage, survive, and succeed at best. But, God has His sights higher than giving you success. He wants to give you redeeming victory.

In Acts 1, Jesus appeared before His people after His resurrection for a period of forty days. It's glorious. I am sure the disciples were hyped. However, over a meal, Jesus gave them a strange command. He told them to wait, to wait in Jerusalem, and to wait for a gift. And, of course, they wanted to know when and how.

To this, Jesus replied, "It is not for you to know the times or dates the Father has set by his own authority," (Acts 1:7). They were basically commanded to wait without knowing, without understanding.

When we are faithful in the waiting, we are testifying to the world that our breakthrough is God's job. It is ever so humbling to admit that your destiny and desire are not in your own hands. Most people in the secular world may refute that belief, but when you believe in God you are also admitting that you yourself are not God. It is then when you can resonate with the psalmist that said in Psalm 31:15, "My times are in your hands…"

Everyone is anxious for a newer and better season to come their way. When those hopes and changes haven't been fulfilled, there's a temptation to walk away from God. I have witnessed people leave the church because certain prophetic words were left unfulfilled for too long. Young people turned to promiscuity in fear that that was the only way to find the right "one". Mothers waited for that sense of kingdom calling again, only to be burned out by the day-to-day demands of raising children and running a home. You want out. You want different. You want better, and the waiting is beginning to feel like God abandoned you.

Yet, after the believers in Acts 1 diligently waited, the Lord delivered what He had promised. The Holy Spirit came, and the first church was born. I would have loved to been there — about 120 actually were. However, the most fascinating part was that Jesus actually showed Himself to over 500 men and women (1 Cor. 15:6). That means approximately 380 people who did not partake in the waiting were also not present for the promise fulfilled. They weren't there to receive the baptism of the Holy Spirit and witness the supernatural manifestation of His gifts. They weren't there to get launched off to the ends of the earth!

The waiting season is an active season. It is not to be mistaken as a time when nothing happens. The believers were not idle as they stayed in Jerusalem and waited for the promise. No, during this unique interim, the believers constantly gathered to pray. They recalled relevant Scripture and obeyed the word. They established a leadership structure to ready themselves for when God's gift would unction them to go to the ends of the earth. In the midst of that, God did not abandoned them. In fact, He was preparing them.

Let's make Jesus famous in our waiting. As your circumstances look dire and your life seems stagnant, may the world see your spirit of thanksgiving. May they hear your praises. For the Lord will indeed do something, and when that something happens, others around you will know exactly who deserves the credit.

Faith Eury Cho has a burning passion to serve as a voice to the voiceless. She serves as a co-pastor alongside her husband at the new church plant, The Presence Church. Faith is the founder of The Honor Summit, a nonprofit organization that is driven to refresh and empower Christian women all around the world. Her most precious role, however, is being a mom to her four children.

The Gifts of the Christ Child - January 4

by Paula Mitchell

*"Above all else, know this: Be prepared at all times for the gifts of God
and be ready always for new ones. For God is a thousand times more ready to
give than we are to receive."*
~Meister Eckhart[53]

Wilkie Au and Noreen Cannon in their book, *Urgings of the
Heart*, write, "Living in an achievement-oriented society, many of us
are influenced by an achievement-oriented spirituality, in which there
is no place for receiving. We resist being indebted and insist on
working for whatever we get. This attitude stands in the way of our
receiving from God, who continually invites us to draw near to obtain
what we need."[54]

For many of us this achievement-oriented spirituality keeps us
from drawing near to receive God's gifts. What's so remarkable about
the amazing events of the first Christmas is that the participants in
God's story, the birth of Jesus, draw near to receive the gifts of the
Child Christ. Mary, after questioning how this can be, responds to the
angel Gabriel's message declaring, "I'm the Lord's maid, ready to
serve"… "let it be with me as you say." (Lk 1:38 The Message). She
ponders God's unexpected gift, proclaiming, He "has done great
things for me" (Lk 1:49 The Voice). Joseph sets aside his dreams in
order to be open to God's invitation to a life radically different from
his wildest expectations.

The gift of silence taught Zechariah to receive a son destined to
prepare the way for the Lord. Elizabeth receives God's mercy in taking
away the stigma of being barren. Zechariah announces God's kindness
in sending a light from heaven to guide us to the path of peace. Simeon
and Anna, prepared by God's Spirit, draw near and literally receive
the infant Jesus, God's promised Messiah. Humble shepherds rejoice
with the angels at his birth. The sight of his star fills the wise men with
indescribable joy as they bow and worship Christ the newborn king.

Invited to draw near and participate in God's salvation plan, they
say, "yes" and receive the gifts of the Child Christ, God's unasked for,

172

unlikely gift to the world. Saying "yes," meant letting go of their hopes and dreams, plans and security, in order to consent to something bigger than what they could see, understand, or even imagine.

We, too, can draw near and wait with a sense of expectation and wonder for God to open us up to new life. Invited by God to let go of our achievement-oriented spirituality, we prepare our hearts to receive God's gifts at Christmas. "Christmas is a gift of love wrapped in human flesh and tied securely with the strong promises of God. It is more than words can tell, for it is a matter for the heart to receive, believe and understand."[55] Invited to receive the gift of God's love, wrapped in the vulnerability of human flesh, we experience God's tender mercy in sending us light to dispel the darkness of sin and death. "For a child is born to us, a son is given to us. The government will rest on his shoulders. And he will be called: Wonderful Counselor, Mighty God, Everlasting Father, **Prince of Peace**." (Isa. 9:6 NLT).

As we receive the gifts of the Child Christ, God gives us a deeper experience of his kindness, love, mercy and grace. We begin to understand, "For God is working in you, giving you the desire and the power to do what pleases him" (Phil. 2:13 NLT). In trusting that God is at work, we learn it's not so much about what we do, instead it's about what **God** is doing in and through us. Trust creates in us a receptive openness to God's Spirit. Focused on Christ, we are invited to participate in **his** redemptive work in our homes, neighborhoods, city and world. We share the amazing good news, "For God wanted them to know that the riches and glory of Christ are for you Gentiles, too. And this is the secret: Christ lives in you. This gives you assurance of sharing his glory." (Col. 1:27 NLT). Christ in you, God's amazing gift to the world!

"Go now into the world, carrying Christmas with you into everyday life. Open the inn within you and make room for that Gift of gifts, even our Lord Jesus Christ".[56]

Paula Mitchell is a spiritual director who lives in Sequim Washington. She is the founder and executive director of Doorways Ministries providing days of prayer, three and five day Ignatian retreats, and a 9-month online program based on the Spiritual Exercises of St. Ignatius. Paula teaches and supervises for the Christian Formation and Direction Ministry training program for Spiritual Directors as well as co-leads their Supervision training program.

Welcoming the Child the Whole World Longs to See - January 5

by Christine Sine

I love images that help us understand the Jesus story from the perspective of different cultures. Several years ago, I came across an interesting photo in the Huffington post article, "Muslim "Last Supper" Photo Offers Interfaith Tribute to Da Vinci's Masterpiece". It made me think even more deeply about the face of Jesus and how, not just we but people of other cultures and faiths see him.

The organizer, Fatima Ali commented,

> "For this year's photo, we wanted to do something that, in its own humble way, aimed to bridge the gap between Eastern and Western cultural and religious norms. We looked up the painting, assigned each person a character, and meticulously tried to mimic the image, while also making it our own."[57]

The pictured group enjoyed the process of putting a different spin on the the iconic artwork. "Most of the people pictured in this photo have been active members of the Islamic Center at NYU[58], and I think one of the greatest values we all have shared is this overwhelming sense of community and religious unity," Ali said. "I don't mean just Muslim unity or Muslim community, I mean on a more universal level, being respectful and considerate of all faiths and religious communities."[59]

Not surprisingly, the photo elicited a varied response from Christians. Some are delighted by this depiction of Christ and his followers with faces that look more authentic than the white faces we usually see. Others are appalled by Muslims depicting what they view as a sacred Christian event.

Why am I sharing about the photo of the Last Supper, you may ask, when we are getting ready to celebrate the birth of Christ? Aren't I

174

getting to the end of the story before we have seen the beginning? No. In so many ways, this photo epitomizes Christmas. When I first posted this, also in the Christmas season, I added a quote from *Monastery Journey to Christmas* by Brother Victor-Antoine D'Avila-Latourrette. He writes, "Jesus is the Prince of Peace whose face the whole world longs to see"[60]. I think that in the hearts of all humankind there is indeed a deep ache for the coming of a saviour. More than that, there is a deep ache to see the face of Jesus in the faces and actions of his followers, and in the faces of all who long for peace where there is violence, abundance where there is starvation and healing where there is disease.

As I look out at my seemingly dead Seattle garden, wet and soggy after another storm, I can fully appreciate this. Winter seems to have destroyed all life, yet hidden in the earth, the roots still live, growing stronger, reaching deeper, ready to emerge in the coming spring. For the Jewish people, there was a long winter of centuries before Jesse's Root, sprouted forth with the coming of Christ, the Messiah. For us, there have been even more centuries of longing, of hoping and of anticipation.

When Christ first appeared, he was like the first sprouts of spring growth — weak, vulnerable, and tiny compared to the tree that would grow. This is the Christ whose remembrance we celebrate at Christmas. Yet, in that tiny shoot, lay the hope and promise of what was and still is to come — a tree that could spread over all the earth, a saviour for the whole world whose power and scope is far greater than any of us could ever imagine. This is the Christ for whose coming we wait with joyful anticipation. This is the Christ whose tree has already spread across the whole earth, yet we still see so much of the darkness that it is meant to overcome. We still wait in anticipation for the full unveiling of this Christ who fills our hearts with longing for the future in which all things will be made new. In the meantime, it is wonderful to catch glimpses of it in the depiction of Christ's birth from many cultures.

I love what Brueggemann says about the coming of Christ:

> There was something unroyal about him: no pretense, no ambition, no limousine no army, no coercion, no royal marking.

Wise and intelligent people are turned toward the regal. Kings and prophets want to penetrate the mystery. But the Jesus who showed up amid royal hopes and royal songs was of another ilk, **powerful in weakness, rich in poverty, wise in foolishness,** confounding the wisdom of the Greeks and bewildering the Jews.

He is beyond all usual categories of power, because he embodies the gentle, gracious, resilient, demanding power of God. He does not trifle in temples and cities and dynasties but in the power and truth of the creator God.[61]

This tender shoot, this vulnerable child, whose very birth reveals the upside down nature of God's kingdom, is an ensign for the nations, a flag towards which all people will be drawn and that includes the Muslims and people of other faiths. The word we translate as "nations" had a very different meaning for the Jews. "Gentiles" were everyone who was not Jewish. It encompassed all peoples outside Israel, opening God's promise of salvation to all cultures and countries. The new kingdom Christ ushered in is open to the entire world. Christ the Messiah, the tiny Branch which is slowly becoming a mighty tree will break down walls and barriers between all people.

Christine describes herself as a contemplative activist, passionate gardener, author, and liturgist. She is the founder of Godspace and her most recent book is The Gift of Wonder: Creative Practices for Delighting in God.

Epiphany: The Light Shines to All Nations – January 6

by Lynne Baab

"Wow, I just had an epiphany," someone says.

"What's that?" a friend responds.

"You know, a bit of a revelation. I suddenly see something in a new light . . ."

As we celebrate the Christian feast day of Epiphany, it is helpful to consider the parallels between the common use of the word "epiphany" and the historic Christian understanding of Epiphany connected to the story of the Magi, or wise men.

An epiphany is a revelation or manifestation of something previously hidden or unclear. At Epiphany we remember that God revealed something through the magi that was previous hidden. What previously hidden thing are we talking about?

Throughout the Old Testament, God desired that the people of Israel be a "light to the nations." In one of the Servant Songs in Isaiah, God says, "I will give you as a light to the nations, that my salvation may reach to the end of the earth" (Isa. 49:6 NRSV). Solomon's prayer at the dedication of the Temple vividly but briefly reflects God's concern for the whole earth. Solomon prays for foreigners who will come to the Temple to pray, asking that God would answer their prayers so that, "all peoples of the earth may know your name" (2 Chron. 6:32-33 NRSV). If you have any doubt that God's intent from the beginning was to enfold all people, read Psalm 96 and count the number of times all the peoples of the earth are mentioned.

God desired that the people of Israel make known to the nations God's power and love. The people of Israel hardly ever rose to the task. In fact, they kept God's love for the nations hidden, either through willful disobedience or through lack of understanding of the significance of the truth they had been entrusted with.

In Christ, this hidden love of God for all people would be revealed more fully, and the first hint of that revelation is the arrival of the magi. The story of the magi in Matthew 2:1-12, gives a glimmer of God's intent that Jesus, this incarnate God, would fulfill Israel's purpose of being a light to the nations.

The magi were Gentiles. They came from "the East," possibly from what is now Saudi Arabia or Iran. They were not people who worshipped the one true God; instead they were astrologers who looked to the stars for guidance. The people of Israel had not fulfilled God's purpose to be a light to the nations, so the stars spoke to the magi about the significance of the birth of this baby!

At Jesus' baptism in the temple, the beautiful old man Simeon understood the significance for all nations of this baby. Simeon says, "For my eyes have seen your salvation that you have prepared in the presence of all peoples, a light for revelation to the Gentiles and for glory to your people Israel" (Lk 2:30-32 ESV).

The notion of light appears so frequently in these stories. The wise men travel by the light of a star. The nation of Israel was called to be a light to the nations. Simeon sees that Jesus will be that light, foreshadowing Jesus' words about being the light of the world (Jn 8:12). And part of the meaning of the word "epiphany" is to see things in a new light. The light of Jesus, revealed at Epiphany, highlights something that had been hidden: God loves all the people, of all the nations, on earth.

I invite you to spend some time reflecting on this year.

- Did you see anything about God in a new light?
- Did you see anything new about God's love for all nations?
- For next year, what would you like to pray for with respect to God's light and God's love for all peoples?

Lynne Baab, Ph.D., is a Presbyterian minister who has written widely about Christian spiritual practices, including her books Sabbath Keeping and Fasting. For information about Lynne's books and to read her weekly blog posts focused on Christian spirituality, visit lynnebaab.com.

Christmas Creed

I believe in Jesus Christ and in the beauty of the gospel begun in Bethlehem.
I believe in the one whose spirit glorified a little town;
and whose spirit still brings music to persons all over the world,
in towns both large and small.
I believe in the one for whom the crowded inn could find no room,
and I confess that my heart still sometimes wants to exclude Christ from my life today.
I believe in the one whom the rulers of the earth ignored
and the proud could never understand;
whose life was among common people,
whose welcome came from persons of hungry hearts.
I believe in the one who proclaimed the love of God to be invincible:
I believe in the one whose cradle was a mother's arms,
whose modest home in Nazareth had love for its only wealth,
who looked at persons and made them see what God's love saw in them,
who by love brought sinners back to purity,
and lifted human weakness up to meet the strength of God.
I confess my ever-lasting need of God:
The need of forgiveness for our selfishness and greed,
the need of new life for empty souls, the need of love for hearts grown cold.
I believe in God who gives us the best of himself.
I believe in Jesus, the son of the living
God, born in Bethlehem this night, for me and for the world.

(by Walter Russell Bowie, copyright unknown)

Resources

Resources for Celtic Advent

- _Celtic Advent: Forty Days of Devotions to Christmas_ by David Cole.
- _A Fragrant Offering: A Daily Prayer Cycle in the Celtic Tradition_ – John Birch. I found it to be an excellent resource to use for the season. Read more of John Birch's resources at: http://www.faithandworship.com/Advent/Advent_Celtic_Christian_Celebration.htm#ixzz2DLSEmYtl
- Celts to the Creche – Brenda Griffin Warren is another Godspace regular. I love this collection of daily devotions that can be accessed daily on her site.
- _The Soul's Slow Ripening: 12 Celtic Practices for Seeking the Sacred_ by Christine Valters Paintner. This is not an Advent book but it is a wonderful book to use for contemplative reflection with a Celtic focus. I have been using it over the last few months and have found much inspiration from it.
- _Journey To The Manger with Patrick and Friends_ by Jean McLachlan Hess.
- The idea of Jesus in the Mess, is from a prayer station in the Christmas Incarnation Sacred Space Prayer Experience at Freerangeworship.com by Lilly Lewin
- PDF Calendar for Celtic Advent and Beyond from Contemplative Cottage

Godspace Resources for Advent and Christmas

Godspace Resource Page: www.godspacelight.com/resources

- Check out our Church Calendar page on Godspace for resource lists, books, and activities for the season.
- Need holiday recipes? Have a look at our recipes on our Hospitality page on Godspace

- <u>Color Your Way Through Advent and Christmas</u> - free download. Includes images and scriptures for colouring during the seasons of Advent and Christmas.
- <u>Advent in a Jar</u> - free download. This fun for the whole family packet is filled with printable "sticks" of activities and instructions for creating your advent jar.
- Advent Prayer Cards - downloadable, 1 set or 3 sets available for purchase in <u>our store</u>. They begin with Celtic Advent so there are 6 for Advent, 1 for Christmas Eve, 4 for the Christmas season and 1 for the Eve of Epiphany.
- <u>An Advent Liturgy by Emma Morgan</u> - This beautiful and creative series of Advent candle liturgies will allow for stories to be shared and prayers to be given and placed.
- *A Journey Toward Home: Soul Travel from Advent to Lent* - This guide approaches the rich seasons of Advent to Lent playfully, yet with yearning and determination. Words ancient and new, stories for the young and old, engage readers in this annual unfolding of miracles and mystery.
- *Waiting for the Light: An Advent Devotional* - It is more than a devotional; it is a complete guide to the Advent and Christmas season, providing liturgies, weekly activities, and daily reflections to equip and nourish us all through the season.
- *Living the Season Well - Reclaiming Christmas* by Jody Collins. She writes, "I am convinced we can reclaim Christmas from the frenzy of gift-giving and presents it has become and mark it by savoring the presence of God and the people in our lives." Practical and engaging book!
- <u>Advent Waiting Prayer Experience</u> by Lilly Lewin. For purchase and download through <u>FreeRange Worship</u>. The Kits come with a leader's guide, supply lists, and photos of how to set up the prayer stations. Along with all the instructions are PDF signs to print out for each station.
- <u>Podcast on Developing a Christmas Passion</u> by John Lewis and his wife, Carissa. Also, check out John's book, <u>Finding the Treasures in Christmas: A Guide to Celebrating Advent for Families with Young Children</u>.
- <u>The Baby Lotion Station</u> found in the Christmas <u>Incarnation Sacred Space Prayer Experience</u> by Lilly Lewin

181

Homemade Cinnamon Christmas Decorations

INGREDIENTS
- 1 cup applesauce
- 1-1 1/4 cup 130 grams ground cinnamon
- 1 tablespoon ground cloves (optional — smells amazing)

INSTRUCTIONS
1. Preheat oven to 200 degrees F. Line a sheet pan with parchment paper.
2. In the bowl of a stand mixer fitted with a paddle attachment, combine the applesauce, cinnamon, and cloves (if using). You want the dough to be able to form a ball without being too sticky. Add additional applesauce or cinnamon if needed. You can also mix the dough by hand.
3. Sprinkle a clean surface with cinnamon (like you would with flour while rolling out cookies). Place the dough on the surface and sprinkle with more cinnamon. Use a rolling pin to roll the dough to 1/4 inch thick, sprinkling with more cinnamon to keep from sticking.
4. Cut out into desired shapes and place on the prepared sheet pan so that they aren't touching. Use a skewer to poke a hole into each ornament (to attach string through). Bake in the preheated oven for 1 1/2 - 2 hours or until rock hard.
5. Loop a decorative string through the ornament and hang on your tree.

How to Make Chai Tea
Yield: Approximately one quart of chai concentrate
INGREDIENTS

- 6 cups water
- 1/3 cup raw sugar/sucanat, or natural sweetener of your choice
- 2 to 3" fresh ginger, sliced
- 5 cinnamon sticks
- 1 teaspoon peppercorns
- 2 vanilla beans
- 3 star anise
- 15 cloves
- 5 allspice (optional)
- 2 teaspoons cardamom seeds
- 5 black tea bags
- Milk of your choice

INSTRUCTIONS

1. In a medium pot, bring the water and sweetener to a boil and simmer until the sweetener is fully dissolved.
2. Add all of the spices, and continue to simmer on low heat for 20 minutes.
3. Remove the mixture from the heat, add the tea bags, and let them steep for 10 minutes.
4. Strain out the spices and tea bags and store your chai concentrate in the fridge (it will last for several weeks)
5. To serve: Mix the chai concentrate 1:1 with milk. Gently heat in a small saucepan until it reaches the desired temperature. Pour into your favourite mug and enjoy. Optional: Add honey to taste.

Chocolate Brownie

Serves 24

INGREDIENTS

450 g butter
400 g dark chocolate (50%+ dark/bittersweet is good)
4 cups sugar
8 eggs
2 ½ tsp vanilla essence
3 cups gluten-free plain flour (normal flour works, but GF makes fudgier brownies)
1 cup cocoa
2 cups nuts (optional, walnuts/macadamias)
Icing sugar to dust

INSTRUCTIONS

Melt butter, chocolate and sugar in a saucepan over a low heat. Remove from heat and leave to cool.

[Egg pro tips: if you don't let the chocolate cool enough there's a risk of scrambling egg in your brownie mix. I recommend breaking the eggs into a cup and adding them one at a time to the mixture; this way if there's anything wrong with that egg or some shell falls in, it's not affecting your whole mixture. Put the empty half eggshells inside each other so you don't get confused about how many you've added!]

Mix the eggs in one at a time, beating well between each addition.

Sieve the flour and cocoa into a separate bowl. Fold these into the chocolate mixture and finally add the vanilla.

Pour into a parchment-lined roasting pan.

Bake in a moderate oven at 180C/350F for 35 minutes.

Sieve icing sugar over once cool then cut.

Other Godspace Resources

The Gift of Wonder by Christine Sine. The Gift of Wonder encouraging us to develop fresh spiritual practices that engage all our senses and help us to live a new kind of spiritual life that embraces the wonder and joy that God intends for us.

Return to Our Senses: Reimagining How We Pray by Christine Sine. Shows you how simple experiences — breathing, drinking a glass of water, walking amongst trees, shooting a photo, picking up a stone — can become "thin places" and pregnant moments in your daily life — helping you awaken to God's presence, savor God's nearness, and translate your experience of God into prayerful, compassionate action.

Rest in the Moment: Reflections for Godly Pauses by Christine Sine. The twelve meditations in this beautiful full-color book are designed to provide moments of refreshment throughout the day or week. The blending together of prayers, reflections, questions and photos invite us to pause, reset and refresh ourselves

To Garden With God by Christine Sine. This resource mixes practical advice with spiritual reflections on the interactions between God's story and our activity in the garden. It is available in both e-book and book form.

Light for the Journey by Christine Sine. This book of morning and evening prayers walks us through the week with a different theme for each day of the week.

Prayer cards available in print and digital formats through our Godspace store.

Godspace is continually developing new resources intended to help inspire our imaginations and create new expressions of life and faith for the future. Check out the books, prayer cards, digital versions, and free downloads available in our store at godspacelight.com.

About the Compilers

Christine Sine

Contemplative activist, passionate gardener, author, and liturgist, Christine loves messing with spiritual traditions and inspiring followers of Jesus to develop creative approaches to spirituality that intertwine the sacred through all of life. She is the founder and facilitator for the popular contemplative blog, godspacelight.com. Her most recent book is *The Gift of Wonder: Creative Practices for Delighting in God*. (IVP 2019)

You can connect with her on
Twitter: https://twitter.com/ChristineSine
Facebook: https://www.facebook.com/christine.sine
Instagram: https://www.instagram.com/christine.sine/
Pinterest: https://www.pinterest.com/christinesine/
Youtube: https://www.youtube.com/user/Christinesine

Lisa DeRosa

Lisa DeRosa loves God and seeks to follow Jesus in whatever way he leads her. She and her husband live with a small intentional community, called The Mustard Seed House, where they share weekly meals, garden together and serve each other as needs arise. She assists Tom and Christine Sine with their businesses and websites, GodspaceLight.com and NewChangemakers.com.

Endnotes:

1 Taken from https://www.faithandworship.com/Advent/
Advent_Celtic_Christian_Celebration.htm#gsc.tab=0
Under Creative Commons License: Attribution, no changes made.

2 David Cole, *Celtic Advent: 40 days of devotions to Christmas,* (Abingdon,
UK: The Bible Reading Fellowship, 2018), 55, Kindle.

3 Archbishop Desmond Tutu and The Dalai Lama, *The Book of Joy:
Lasting Happiness in a Changing World,* (New York, NY: Avery; Later prt.
Edition, 2016), 59.

4 https://godspacelight.com/2018/06/27/27740/

5 Taken from: *Advent In Narnia: Reflections for the Season,* Heidi
Haverkamp, © 2015 by Heidi Haverkamp. Used by Permission of
Westminster John Knox Press.

6 https://godspacelight.com/2013/11/19/creating-an-advent-prayer-
garden/

7 Extract from *Living the Season Well-Reclaiming Christmas,* Jody Collins
© 2017 (original) by Jody Collins. Used with permission by Jody
Collins.

8 From *On The Brink of Everything: Grace, Gravity, and Getting
Old,* copyright © 2018 by Parker Palmer, Berrett-Koehler Publishers,
Inc., San Francisco, CA. All rights reserved. www.bkconnection.com

9 Excerpted from *The Soul's Slow Ripening: 12 Celtic Practices for Seeking
the Sacred,* by Christine Valters Painter. Copyright 2018 by Ave Maria
Press, P.O. Box 428, Notre Dame, IN 46556. Used with permission of
the publisher.

10 https://godspacelight.com/2017/06/28/spiritual-retreats-
powerful-tools-to-increase-our-faith/

11 https://godspacelight.com/2016/07/19/the-web-of-friendship-2/

12 Taken from *Anam Cara: A Book Of Celtic Wisdom* by John O'Donohue. xvii. Copyright © 1997 by John O'Donohue. Used by permission of HarperCollins Publishers. www.harpercollins.com/.

13 O'Donohue, Ibid.

14 https://godspacelight.com/shop/advent-in-a-jar/

15 https://www.faithandworship.com/
Celtic_Blessings_and_Prayers.htm#gsc.tab=0

16 Adapted from Ray Simpson of Lindisfarne, author of *Tree of Life: Celtic Prayers to the Universal Christ* (Anamchara Books, 2020), used with permission.

17 Taken from *Windows of the Soul: Hearing God in the Everyday Moments of Your Life* by Ken Gire. Copyright © 1996 by Ken Gire, Jr.. Used by permission of Zondervan. www.zondervan.com

18 Joe E. Pennel, Jr., *The Whisper of Christmas*, (Nashville, TN: Upper Room Books, 1984), 61.

19 Mary and Joseph by Rip Caswell - https://caswellsculptures.com/
product/mary-and-joseph-monument/

20 Kenneth Bailey, *Jesus Through Middle Eastern Eyes*, (Downers Grove, IL: IVP Academic, 2008), 45.

21 Bailey, Ibid, 46.

22 Bailey, Ibid, 46.

23 https://www.learnreligions.com/symbolic-colors-of-advent-700445

24 https://godspacelight.com/2015/11/19/advent-candle-liturgy-emma-morgan/

25 Taken from: https://globalworship.tumblr.com/post/
169117941855/a-toast-to-the-mystery-of-the-incarnation-in-the?, used with permission by Father Kenneth Tanner.

[26] Gerald May, *The Dark Night of the Soul*, (New York, NY: HarperCollins Publishers, 2004), 197.

[27] "Jesus Bids Us Shine", words by Susan Bogert Warner and music by Edwin Othello Excell

[28] Pete Greig, dirtyglory.org

29 Goodrick, Edward W., and John R. Kohlberger III, *The Strongest NIV Exhaustive Concordance*, (Grand Rapids, MI: Zondervan).

[30] "Come Thou Unexpected Jesus", https://youtu.be/vRAFQCOkjgE.

[31] https://www.circlewood.online/

[32] Excerpt from her devotional, *Catching the Light* by Jenneth Graser. Used with permission.

[33] Taken from *PRAISE!* by Mary Harwell Sayler, published by Cladach Press. Used with permission.

[34] Global Christian Worship: https://globalworship.tumblr.com/

[35]John O'Donohue, *Beauty: The Invisible Embrace*, (New York, NY: Harper Perennial Perennial ed. Edition, 2005), 84.

[36] Google search: images of Jesus site:globalworship.tumblr.com

[37] To read more about this article: https://www.abc.net.au/news/2018-07-11/australians-involved-with-thai-cave-rescue-dr-richard-harris/9978700

[38] Taken from *Theologian of the Graced Search for Meaning* by Karl Rahner. © 1992 by Karl Rahner. Used with permission by Augsburg Fortress. www.augsburgfortress.org/.

[39] https://info.franciscanmedia.org/advent-with-richard-rohr-pillar

[40] Rahner, Ibid.

[41] "If you're missing someone this Christmas this song's dedicated to you" - The Piano Guys ft Craig Aven, https://youtu.be/0yFXfAGl17M

42 Casting Crowns, *Somewhere In Your Silent Night*, https://youtu.be/nT-5cP4BeoI

43 If you are looking for a liturgy for Blue Christmas, check this one out: http://sacraparental.com/2014/12/23/a-blue-christmas-service-if-youre-hurting-at-christmas/.

44 "The Work of Christmas" and "Christmas is Waiting to be Born" are from Howard Thurman's *The Mood of Christmas and Other Celebrations* and is used by permission of Friends United Press. All rights reserved.

45 Lucy Maud Montgomery, *Emily of New Moon*, (London, UK: Virago Press, 2013, *originally published in 1923*), 8. Usable under fair use: https://journaloflmmontgomerystudies.ca/open-access-and-copyright.

46 Kenneth Bailey, *Jesus Through Middle Eastern Eyes*, (Downers Grove, IL: IVP Academic, 2008), 28.

47 Bailey, Ibid, 54.

48 jonhuckins.net/the-global-immersion-project/

49 https://globalimmerse.org/

50 Jon Huckins, author of *Mending the Divides: Creative Love in a Conflicted World*

51 https://godspacelight.com/2016/01/01/what-name-would-we-give-jesus/

52 Some of the books and resources available on the power of our thinking: Joyce Meyer – The Battlefield of the Mind, Steve & Wendy Backlund – Igniting Hope, and Dr Caroline Leaf – Switch on Your Brain

53 https://www.purposefairy.com/81964/31-life-changing-lessons-to-learn-from-meister-eckhart/

[54] Excerpt from *Urgings of the Heart: A Spirituality of Integration*, by Wilkie Au and Noreen Cannon, copyright © 1995 by Wilkie Au and Noreen Cannon, published by Paulist Press, Inc., New York/Mahwah, NJ. www.paulistpress.com.

[55] Frank McKibben, original source unknown, http://www.photo-party-favors.com/Christian-Christmas-quotes.html.

[56] Ann Barr Weems, *Reaching for Rainbows: Resources for Creative Worship,* © 1980. Used by Permission of Westminster John Knox Press.

[57] Yasmine Hafiz, "Muslim 'Last Supper' Photo Offers Interfaith Tribute To Da Vinci's Masterpiece", *Huff Post*, December 6, 2017. https://www.huffpost.com/entry/muslim-last-supper-photo_n_4455289?

[58] www.icnyu.org/

[59] Hafiz, Ibid.

[60] Brother Victor-Antoine D'Avila-Latourrette, *Monastery Journey to Christmas,* (Liguori, MO: Liguori Publications, October 1, 2011).

[61] Walter Brueggemann, *Celebrating Abundance: Devotions for Advent,* © 2017. Used by Permission of Westminster John Knox Press.

Printed in Great Britain
by Amazon